Not The One. A Woman's Guide To Identifying Red Flags

Stina Sanders

Legal disclaimer

Dedicated to those who inspired this book and will probably say it's not about them.

It is.

CONTENTS

CHAPTER 2 - DATING APPS

RED FLAG 12: His profile has little information about him
RED FLAG 13: His selfies are topless
RED FLAG 14: The 'must haves' profile
RED FLAG 15: He's too good to be true
RED FLAG 16: He's suggestive
RED FLAG 17: He takes a long time to message
RED FLAG 18: He's too keen to meet you
RED FLAG 19: He's hesitant to meet you
RED FLAG 20: He keeps his dating profile active...even after making it exclusive with

CHAPTER 3 - THE FIRST DATE

RED FLAG 21: He's late to your date...and doesn't tell you
RED FLAG 22: He looks terrible
RED FLAG 23: He's rude to waiters
RED FLAG 24: He's isn't present
RED FLAG 25: He love bombs
RED FLAG 26: He's derogatory
RED FLAG 27: He's sarcastic and makes too many jokes

RED FLAG 28: He admits he doesn't want a girlfriend
RED FLAG 29: He says: "Your place or mine?"
RED FLAG 30: He doesn't make plans to see you again

CHAPTER 4 - SOCIAL MEDIA

RED FLAG 31: He's always online
RED FLAG 32: He follows a lot of bikini models and Only Fans girls
RED FLAG 33: The same women like and comment on his posts
RED FLAG 34: He doesn't follow you or interact with your posts
RED FLAG 35: His DM replies are flirty
RED FLAG 36: He airs his dirty laundry and fights online
RED FLAG 37: He doesn't post you on his social media after months of dating
RED FLAG 38: You stalk him online

CHAPTER 5 - COMMUNICATION

RED FLAG 39: He says "I love you" too soon
RED FLAG 40: He texts too much

RED FLAG 41: He rarely texts or calls (but is always on his phone)
RED FLAG 42: He doesn't listen to you
RED FLAG 43: He brings up your faults or past mistakes
RED FLAG 44: He never says sorry
RED FLAG 45: He lies
RED FLAG 46: He isn't transparent
RED FLAG 47: He only calls you at night or when he's drunk
RED FLAG 48: He makes you feel like you're treading on eggshells

CHAPTER 6 - EXES

RED FLAG 49: He's not over his ex
RED FLAG 50: He talks about his ex all the time
RED FLAG 51: He refuses to talk about his ex, full stop
RED FLAG 52: He compares you to his ex
RED FLAG 53: He's friends with his ex
RED FLAG 54: He says his ex is a psycho or crazy

CHAPTER 7 - SEX

RED FLAG 55: Sex with you is more important than getting to know you
RED FLAG 56: He pressures you to have sex
RED FLAG 57: He's selfish in bed
RED FLAG 58: He becomes distant after sex

CHAPTER 8: INSECURITIES, MANIPULATION & CONTROL

RED FLAG 59: He gets angry easily
RED FLAG 60: He makes you feel insecure
RED FLAG 61: He checks your phone
RED FLAG 62: He's a jealous guy
RED FLAG 63: His way or the highway
RED FLAG 64: He's controlling
RED FLAG 65: He gaslights you
RED FLAG 66: He's not supportive
RED FLAG 67: He tests you
RED FLAG 68: He gives you the silent treatment

CHAPTER 9 - MONEY

RED FLAG 69: He lives off the bank of mum and dad
RED FLAG 70: He asks you for money

RED FLAG 71: He is irresponsible with
money
RED FLAG 72: He buys your love
RED FLAG 73: He's not generous
RED FLAG 74: He tells you how successful
he is

CHAPTER 10 - FRIENDS & FAMILY

RED FLAG 75: He hasn't introduced you to
his friends or family
RED FLAG 76: He hates your friends and
family
RED FLAG 77: He doesn't respect your
privacy
RED FLAG 78: He prioritises his friends
over you
RED FLAG 79: Your friends and family hate
him
RED FLAG 80: He's overly attached to his
family
RED FLAG 81: He hates his family

CHAPTER 11: COMMITMENT

RED FLAG 82: He discusses future plans
(without you)

RED FLAG 83: All of his previous relationships have been short or casual
RED FLAG 84: He refuses to be exclusive
RED FLAG 85: He's a flake
RED FLAG 86: He's taken
RED FLAG 87: He doesn't want to get married (but you do)
RED FLAG 88: He doesn't want kids (but you do)

FINAL THOUGHTS

HELP & SUPPORT

PREFACE

I hate prefaces in books. So I don't blame you if you're inclined to skip this one. But I would warn you, this part is sort of imperative for understanding the rest of the book. Sorry.

My name is Stina Sanders and I am a psychodynamic and cognitive behavioural therapist, specialising in relationships and narcissistic abuse recovery. Fancy as that might sound, my background in psychology isn't the reason I decided to write this book. Instead, this book is inspired by my own dating experience.

To give you some context, I'm a survivor of a physically and emotionally abusive relationship. I've also dated narcissists, addicts, not to mention controlling and manipulative individuals. Oh and I nearly forgot - cheaters, liars, f**k boys, time wasters and emotionally unavailable men. Some list, hey?

Before anything gets twisted, I would like to add that I have also dated some wonderful, kind and caring men. But this book isn't about them.

The reason I'm giving you an insight into my dating history is because I don't want anyone reading this book to feel like I'm judging your life choices – so please know that I'm not. Any mistake you've made, there's a really solid chance that I've made it too.

So back to me collecting red flags like I was playing some sort of dating version of Pokémon Go. It wasn't until I entered my thirties, that I realised something had to change. And painful as it was to admit, that something, was me.

Instead of doing the sensible thing and saying 'bye' as soon as a red flag appeared, I always took the Spanish bull approach, and charged towards them. This was partly down to me not trusting my own judgment and because I'm a hopeless romantic who believes in the fairytale ending. Anyone who showed me a bit of attention, I grabbed hold of it.

After extensive therapy for myself, I realised that if I did want to end up in a happy and safe relationship then my acceptance for red flags had to stop. I had to stop making excuses for people's poor behaviour and get my sh*t together.

While training as a therapist I not only became self-aware, I also learned a CBT technique which helps to solve problems and find solutions. During my studies, I realised that I could use this technique when it came to my problem of dating red flags. The technique is simple and it involves writing a list of what you want and what you will do to achieve it. By 'do' I mean changing your thoughts and behaviour to get the result that you want. I decided to take this approach to my love life and so I wrote a list of what I wanted in a relationship and person. The list looked a little something like this:

What I want:
1. I want to marry and have children.
2. I want an open and honest relationship where we both share similar values.
3. I want to date a kind, caring, secure, loving and supportive person.
4. I want to date someone who has similar interests and hobbies to me.
5. I want to be with someone who is ambitious, funny and smart.

I then wrote my list of what I didn't want from a relationship. I titled this my deal-breakers list and it looked like this:

Dealbreakers
1. Drug user/dealer
2. Liar
3. Unreliable/irresponsible
4. Emotionally unavailable
5. Jealous or insecure
6. Controlling
7. Not supportive
8. Lazy

Both lists were way longer than that but I won't bore you with all the finer details. Once I had made my lists of wants and don't wants, I made a pact with myself to say 'no' to anyone who ticked a box from my deal breaker list. No matter how attractive they were, or what other fantastic qualities they had, if they ticked a 'no' box, that was it.

I won't lie to you. It can be hard to say 'no' to someone you like. After all, emotions aren't logical. It's hard to not continue meeting or dating someone that you connect with, and it's so tempting to ignore the negative things about them. A lot of us do this. We hope that the positives will outweigh the negatives - we tell ourselves that 'no-one is perfect' and that we're being too picky. And while this may work in the short term, in my experience it never ends well. You can try to paint a red flag green, but underneath it's always going to be a red flag. That's why it's so important to set strong boundaries for yourself and not allow desire to sabotage your happiness. **Ignoring warning signs or dealbreakers is a false economy, it might bring you a relationship in the short term, but it will mean that it takes longer overall to find the right person.**

Of all of the men I've dated who turned out to be bad eggs, it was possible to tell from the outset that it was going to end badly. With each and every one of them I spotted all the red flags from the get-go. My intuition would scream at me that something was off, but sadly time and time again, I would ignore my instinct.

I would love to go back to my younger self and tell her to listen to the little voice that she would regularly hush. I'd love to ask myself, "Are you sure you're OK with that behaviour from him? Like really?'. I wish I had had more confidence and a stronger expectation of how I should be treated. It would have saved me a lot of heartache and time.

That's why I felt obliged to put my experience down in a book. To save someone else from getting hurt, whether that be you or my future daughter. Learn from my mistakes – I can't go back in time and unlive them, but I might be able to help you avoid yours.

You picked up this book either because you're my mum or you're tired of dating red flags and want to learn how to avoid them. Maybe you want clarity that your intuition is right or maybe you just want to be aware of red flags that men can display. Whatever your reason, you've picked the right book.

Firstly, before we divulge into red flags, I would like you to take a moment to analyse your behaviour. Do you often fall in love with someone within the first six months? Do you ignore red flags? Are you flexible with your boundaries and deal breakers? Do you fantasise that the relationship is something that it isn't? Do you cling on to people even when you're not happy, because you're scared of being alone? If you answered yes to any of those questions, it's time for you to take accountability for your behaviour. By not working on yourself will only prevent you from getting what you want.

In order for my methods to work, I suggest that you start working towards two things as of today: self-respect and boundaries.

Self-respect gives you the ability to say 'bye' to anyone who is a deal breaker. And that's an essential part of breaking the cycle. There might be moments in this process where you feel that you are being harsh and that you should give people the benefit of the doubt. Well, maybe you should, but with love: how has that been working out for you so far? Learning where your boundaries lie will enable you to cut relationships off before there's a chance for them to turn toxic. It will stop abusers, time wasters and f**k boys from running rings around you. It will put you in a better position for finding the one.

This book will make you hyper aware of red flags and it will make you self-aware enough to notice when you're letting one slide.

Most importantly I want you to know your own worth. Stick to your guns and refuse to date in a win-lose situation for both you and the gentleman in question. To put it simply, do not entertain anyone who waves a red flag at you. **As soon as you realise you are enough; you will stop welcoming red flags into your life.**

A NOTE ON GENDER & SEXUAL ORIENTATION

I am a hetrosexual female who dates men, so I will be using the gender pronoun he/him/his in this book. Regardless of your sexual orientation and how you identify, I believe the red flags that are outlined in this book can be applied to all people, regardless of gender or sexual orientation. The language choices in this book are intended for simplicity, not erasure.

ACKNOWLEDGMENTS

First and foremost, I would like to thank my dad, Crizzle. Not his real name but my nickname for him. Aside from being the best dad and my favourite human in the world, Crizzle has taught me how to hold my own in a man's world. Although I haven't always listened to his advice, pep talks and wisdom - without him, this book would never have been written. I love you very much and thank you for teaching me everything that I know.

I would also like to thank Rebecca Reid, for editing and proofreading this book. Thank you for all your advice and support.

I want to thank all my friends and family for always being there for me. You have all been my own personal therapist over the years and I'm grateful to have you in my life. Shout out to the Turkey Baster whatsapp group! Callen and Roya, you are both truly amazing friends and I can't thank you enough for always calling me out on my BS and putting a smile on my face.

Finally thank you to my readers. From those that have followed me on Instagram since day dot to those who have just purchased NOT THE ONE. I just want to acknowledge your continuous support online and offline, it really does mean a lot.

INTRODUCTION

It all starts with you. What is it that you want? What are you looking for in a relationship and what type of person works for you?

You may already have an idea of what you want, or you may not. As a therapist the best advice I can give to you when working out your goals, is to write a list. Start with writing a list of everything you want in a partner and relationship. Then write another list, this time writing down all of the things you don't want in a partner and relationship.

Let's start with your green flag list – the list of everything which makes up your perfect partner. In order to make a really comprehensive green flag list, start by imagining your 'perfect' person. If you could wave a wand and conjure them up right now, what would they look like? What do they behave like? Are they sociable? Do they want a family? What are their morals? Beliefs? Are they smart? Do they drink alcohol? Do they exercise regularly? Are they ambitious? How do you feel when you're around them? How would you spend a perfect weekend together?

Grab a pen and paper or open your phone notes and list 20 things that are important to you in a partner. Jot down what you think your ideal relationship looks like. Don't worry if you feel you're being shallow when adding specifics. You're not. This is your life and you can set your standards to whatever you want. Plus, you never have to show this list to anyone, so it can be as 'unreasonable' as you like.

You can call it manifesting, setting an intention, or just focusing your mind – but if you've got a clear idea of what you're aiming for and what you're trying to avoid, you're a lot more likely to achieve it.

Next, write a separate list. This time of all your deal breakers, or as I like to call them, red flags. List at least 20 things that you don't want in a partner and relationship. Take a moment to think about an individual who wouldn't match you and your lifestyle. Think about morals, beliefs and attitudes. If honesty is important to you, then put liars in your red flag list. If you're short of ideas, try reflecting on what hurt you the most in previous relationships and how that hurt might have been avoided if the person in question had behaved differently. Were they controlling? Critical? Unreliable?

In the first instance these lists might not be exhaustive so you may find yourself adding more green and red flags over time. It's important that you regularly refer back to these lists. Especially when you start dating someone. By reminding yourself what you want will stop you from allowing red flags to enter your life, no matter how rich, good looking or funny they are. For example, if your date says they don't like kids but you have two or want kids in the future, you will know that's a dealbreaker. The same applies if your date says that he loves nothing more than to travel and you too love to plane hop. Then this is a tick in your green flag list.

Don't delete anything from the red flag list – you wrote it down for a reason. Especially if you've met someone who might tick a red flag box. We've all been there, but just don't.

I'd also recommend writing your lists on paper and placing them where you will regularly see them just to remind yourself what it is you want and don't want. Think of it as a commitment to yourself, that you won't allow any red flags to enter your life, only green.

The point of the lists is to find a significant other that ticks the majority of boxes in your green flag list and none in the red flag list. Some of you may be thinking 'Well hang on, no one is perfect' and 'why should I let a person pass me by just because they tick one red flag box?'.

You're absolutely right to think that no one is perfect but in my experience, **ignoring red flags will be the reason you breakup later.** It's of course, up to you to prioritise the red flags in your list. It all depends on what you are willing to tolerate but I wouldn't ignore anything that makes you feel uncomfortable. **In your heart of hearts you will know what feels right to you and what you deserve, so never settle for less.**

It's also worth me noting that there is a difference between a manageable character flaw and a red flag. **Your red flag list should be a list of deal breakers, not just a list of things that you find mildly annoying.** Telling you that you look 'slutty' when you're dressed up to go out is a red flag. Not liking Taylor Swift, for instance, – while questionable – is not. By keeping your list of red flags short-ish and specific, you'll avoid conflating minor annoyances with proper red flags.

Keep in mind that turning a blind eye to any red flag can be an error but ignoring some can be extremely dangerous. Especially if the red flags are disrespectful, abusive or toxic.

If you are concerned that you are in an abusive relationship, speak to your GP or see a therapist who can help support you through this process, or if you feel that you're in danger, contact the police. At the back of this book, I have provided some helplines, charities and websites that can give advice if you are in an emotionally or physically abusive situation.

Finding 'the one' has to start with you. This is both good news and bad news. Bad, because it means you can't just wait for love to arrive on your doorstep. Good because it means that you're in control of your destiny.

Recognise what it is you want and push past anyone who doesn't meet your needs. **Always remember: the wrong one gets in the way of the right one.** If your current partner doesn't fit the bill, then ask yourself why are you holding on to a relationship that's not working? If you're not tied to someone by sharing property or having kids together, there's genuinely no reason to stay once you realise that it's not working. Life is short and the time you spend trying to make things work with a red flag is time you will never get back. **Stop wasting your time with people who are incapable of giving you the love you deserve.**

If you are tied to your partner by life commitments, that doesn't mean you need to remain that way for the rest of your life either. Staying in a relationship is a choice.

We must take accountability for our own choices. If you ignore red flags or put yourself in a position that clouds your judgement, then this is your fault. For example, if you've met someone and within 4 months moved in with them, then you are setting yourself up for a fall. Why? Because rushing into a relationship before getting to know someone is likely to end in tears. Sure, you hear the odd story of two people meeting and marrying within a week, then living happily ever after, but these stories are rare. The same goes for women who date a married man, who then leaves his wife to be with them. These women are delusional to not believe he wouldn't do the same and cheat on them! It's through having self-awareness that will stop you from dating red flags. I'm not judging you for behaving colour blind when it comes to red flags, I've been there. But the only person who can stop this pattern is you.

Self-awareness is what will help you to avoid dating red flags. For some of you reading this book, it may be realising that you have codependency issues, and the desire for validation or the need for someone to 'complete' you. When you understand that these needs have a detrimental effect on your relationships, it will be the first step to your self-growth. We all have the power to change our behaviour and thoughts, and it is that power that will serve us well in all avenues of life.

It's natural to feel worried that you're never going to meet someone. When Instagram is wall-to-wall engagement, wedding and pregnancy announcements. Society bombards women with the message that if you don't find someone soon, you'll 'end up' alone.

But trust me, men are like buses. A new one will always come along. The most important thing is that you don't panic, jump on a bus going in the

wrong direction and then waste precious time trying to get back en route.

Go back to your green flag list. Identify your desired man traits and then think strategically about how you're going to meet your green flag guy. If it's important to you that this person is fit and healthy, you're going to have a better chance of meeting him at a running club than at a nightclub. Maybe your desired man is ambitious and in the same career field as you. If so, go to a networking event. Maybe your desired man is a kind and caring soul. If so, why not volunteer with a charity. You have to put yourself out there if you are to meet anyone. That includes your soulmate. Plus, these are all genuinely good, enjoyable ways to use your time.

There's a reason that people so often find a partner when they've stopped looking – it's because there's a lot of fun to be had when you're not scouring Hinge for a partner. Embrace being single and enjoy this journey. When you do meet someone, check your green and red lists to see if your date matches the criteria. Most importantly when it comes to dating, trust your gut.

CHAPTER 1 - THE BASICS

According to scientists, it can take between 90 seconds and 4 minutes to decide if you fancy someone. In my dating heyday, it would usually take me less than a minute of meeting someone to have totally planned our wedding day. Castle venue in the South of France, followed by a huge party with lots of champagne for 400 people, in case you were wondering.

All jokes aside, when we meet someone who we find attractive, it's not uncommon to get swept up in what could be. Unfortunately this lust can affect rationale and weaken our boundaries, making us more susceptible to red flags.

That's why we must keep our high heels firmly on the ground whenever we meet someone new. First impressions are not always what they seem. Narcissists and sociopaths in particular, are very charming people when you first meet them - so don't be fooled by people's masks. It's actually after a few dates or even months later that people begin to show their true selves. Which is why it's important to take your time and get to know people before you commit to any sort of relationship with them.

If at any point when meeting someone for the first time, you hear a little voice in your head

scream *"Ergh no I don't like that"*. **Make a note and review your thoughts later, because that little voice is your intuition screaming 'RED FLAG!'. Listen to it.**

RED FLAG 1: He doesn't respect you

In the words of Aretha Franklin: R-E-S-P-E-C-T

Respect is the most fundamental principle when it comes to any relationship. Without respect, relationships don't work. They become one-sided, fragile and at worst, toxic.

If the guy you're dating doesn't respect you, he doesn't value you. Read that again.

While most of us are able to tell when someone is being disrespectful, especially if the person in question is abusive or disloyal, there are so much more insidious behaviours that shouldn't be ignored. For example,
when your partner doesn't listen or disregards your feelings, that is disrespectful. When your boyfriend continuously breaks promises, that is disrespectful. Crossing your personal boundaries, making fun of your passions and not apologising for their wrongdoings - are all signs of disrespect.

Unfortunately, the tricky thing about disrespect is that it often requires some level of discernment to identify. Of course, as mentioned, you have obvious acts of disrespect, such as verbal and physical attacks, but you may also find yourself in a situation where when you do call out someone for their negative words or digs, they turn around and say, *"You're so sensitive, it was just a joke"*. This instant dismissal usually leads to you feeling more hurt or second-guessing your feelings. *'Maybe he's right, I am being over-sensitive?'*. But you're not being sensitive; your feelings and boundaries are being abused. Making excuses like this not only affects you emotionally, but it lets your partner continue their disrespectful behavior too.

The problem with overlooking or justifying disrespectful behaviour, is when the relationship becomes dangerous territory. This is why it's so important that you set high standards and never allow anyone to disrespect you, your feelings or boundaries.

REG FLAG 2: He's a man-child

It can be hard to spot a man-child initially but sooner or later Peter Pan will appear. Unfortunately many women romanticise the idea of the boy who never grew up. We like to make excuses for his 'childlike' ways, but this will be a heavy price to pay down the road.

When it comes to detecting a man-child, start by asking him about his friends. When he talks about them does he become an adolescent again? Does he tell you a funny story about his mate Mitch, that really isn't that funny? Well, let me tell you, poor Mitch's testicles have never been the same since he stapled his balls to a sofa. Yeah, *really* funny.

Sure we can all be a bit silly at times but observe how a man behaves most of the time. Can he keep to adult limits when it comes to alcohol or does he get wasted and go crazy with cocaine and find himself waking up in an alley? This may work for you, but for anyone looking for a reliable person, this isn't for you.

How does he deal with the responsibilities in his life? Does he turn up for work on time and do his share? Or does he flake and expect other people to pick up the slack? Does he pay his bills on time, keep his home clean, do his own laundry on a reasonable schedule? These things aren't rocket science, but it's amazing how many grown ass men aren't able to do them.

I would approach with caution a man who is dependent on his parents and still living at home. Is he saving for a house deposit? Putting himself through university? Or does he just really like having Mummy iron his pants?

It's also worth observing how he talks about the 'adults' in his life – his parents, grandparents, bosses, any authority figures he's connected with.

Does he respect them? Or does he perceive them as big meanies who are spoiling his fun? If it's the latter, you've quite possibly got yourself an adopted child, not a boyfriend.

The difference between a man and a man-child, is a man is a responsible individual who looks out for you and takes accountability. He makes you feel secure and isn't afraid of adult conversation. A man-child is not responsible. They are men who you will end up mothering and while the thought of looking after someone may excite you, take a minute to realise that mothering doesn't just include caring. It also involves picking up after him, like his mess or paying off his debts.

If he has a fear of commitment, is emotionally unavailable and behaves immaturely, the likelihood is you are dealing with a man-child. So if chasing Peter Pan is not what you want, please may I suggest that you tell him to fuck off back to Neverland?

REG FLAG 3: You have no mutual interests

Having something in common with a partner, friend, colleague or anyone for that matter is what brings two people together. Having mutual interests is what helps us to form a bond. "Ah you like running marathons? Me too!".

Whether that's sharing passions, hobbies, values, likes or dislikes, having common ground allows relationships to build. Although opposites can attract, if you don't have anything in common, then it is likely that you won't have much to share together.

If you're a gym bunny who loves nothing more than to hike up mountains in your spare time, dating someone who hates the thought of just climbing up two flights of stairs, may be a challenge moving forward in your relationship. Not everyone needs to share your interests but it does help when the person you date loves the same things that you do.

The trick to discover if you have mutual interests with someone is to ask them questions. Ask them what they do in their spare time. Do they have any hobbies? What are they passionate about? Quiz them on their music and film taste. Are they a bookworm like you? Is their favourite cuisine the same as yours?

If your date has different interests or passions to you, that's totally OK. Find out what they are and see if you can work with your differences of lifestyle. Maybe you can tolerate an unsociable stamp collector or maybe you draw the line when it comes to someone who only listens to heavy metal music. **In my experience, when lifestyles don't match, it's likely you won't be a match made in heaven in the long run.**

However, for those who don't share your interests but are genuinely interested and supportive, or would like to learn about them, is a good sign. We can't all be the same but it does help if you are on the same page when it comes to having a good time and enjoying yourself.

On a side note, be wary of people who seem too similar to you when you first meet them. Also known as mirroring, mirroring is a manipulation tactic that narcissists and abusers use when pretending to share similar qualities and interests to you. They do this to make you feel connected with them which will ultimately lure you into a false sense of security.

RED FLAG 4: He doesn't initiate dates

There is nothing wrong with you making the first move, but if he isn't initiating dates, then abort mission. This man is clearly busy or tied up with something or someone else. Whether it's work related or another relationship, it is clear he isn't ready to prioritise spending time with you and for that reason he should be left well alone. **If you allow someone to put you at the bottom of their to-do list at the start of the relationship, it's not very likely you'll ever reach the top.**

If you organised the first date, whatever you do, don't take it into your hands and start bombarding him with texts asking if he wants to meet again. He doesn't. If he did he'd be making plans with you. I appreciate my fellow feminists will be cross with me for not encouraging women to make the second move, but when you've already placed all your cards on the table the first time and the other person isn't playing, then there is no game.

If however he has initiated the last couple of dates and everything has been going smoothly, then yes of course, call him up and ask to hang out. If you haven't heard from him since the first date or he's not initiating meeting you, then don't do anything. He knows you're interested, that's why you matched on a dating app or went on a first date together. **Don't chase him.**

People make time for the things they want to do and people value what they regard as difficult to acquire. **If he's interested he'll initiate a date with you, either by phone or messenger pigeon. If he doesn't then park this guy to the side and keep it moving.** The less time you waste here, the quicker you'll get to 'happily ever after'.

RED FLAG 5: He only hangs out with you at night and indoors only

34

Unless you work weird hours, when a guy only wants to hang out with you at night, this is an indication he sees you as a booty call or a barn owl.

To add insult to injury, if he only wants to hang out with you at his or your place, then this is a massive red flag. This screams to me that he doesn't want to be seen in public with you or he just wants one thing and one thing only. I know it's horrible to hear, but it can happen to anyone and it's not a reflection of your worth.

This man should be proud to have you on his arm and show you off to the world. So why are you allowing him to treat you like a lady of the night?

If you find yourself in this situation you need to address the issue upfront and quickly. There could be lots of reasons as to why he only wants to meet you indoors. He might be agoraphobic or broke and can't afford dinner or drinks. Give him the benefit of the doubt and ask him to meet you for a coffee and walk, or alternatively you treat him to dinner and drinks. See how he reacts when you ask to meet in public. If he'd rather keep things behind closed doors, leave him on the other side of the door and walk away.

A serious relationship is all about doing fun activities and exploring the world together. You can't do this in his bedroom. You deserve to be

taken out and treated like a queen in public, day and night.

RED FLAG 6: He forgets your name

We've all been there and called someone a different name. Brain fog, stress or our mind working in overdrive can make us say silly things.

We're only human. We will all make mistakes and the occasional Freudian slip is normal. However if your partner says another woman's name that you haven't heard before or are suspicious of. This is a red flag.

It happened to me when my boyfriend (at the time) was cheating on me. I had a gut feeling that he was up to no good and one day while we were deep into a five hour car journey, he accidentally said a random girl's name instead of mine. His face turned grey and at that moment I just knew he was being unfaithful. Low and behold, a few weeks later, the truth prevailed. My female intuition had been right; he had been cheating on me.

Beware of Freudian slips, they are usually the gateway to the truth.

RED FLAG 7: It's all about him

Have you ever been on a date with someone who only talks about themselves and doesn't ask you any questions? It's so unattractive and just a warning sign that they're not interested in you.

I remember going on a date with a guy who took great pleasure in only talking about himself. At the time I was blind to his lack of interest in me because I was genuinely interested in him. *Get me a sick bucket now*. What's sad is I didn't realise until much later that he didn't care about me, nor did he want to get to know me. Even after months of dating I don't think he even knew what my favourite colour was.

Dating people who are out for themselves is like a constant show. The *'Me, me, me. Let me tell you more about me'* show. **When someone only talks about themself, it is usually because they're not interested in you or have a huge ego.** Help them to see the error of their ways by asking for a refund to their show.

RED FLAG 8: His long-term goals doesn't match yours

We all have different perceptions about what success looks like. How you envision success is different from how I perceive success. This goes for everyone that you will ever meet. You may think success equates to being a millionaire, living in a big house on the hill and driving a Ferrari, whereas someone else might think success is a Hemsworth brother and a beach shack.

That's why it's worth finding someone who is on the same page as you in terms of goals. If for example, you are a career driven woman who has ambitions to meet someone, save and buy a house together, then a slacker who sits on their sofa all day, spending money, playing on his Xbox is likely to be a red flag for you. While there is no judgment for how someone wishes to live their life, it is helpful to find a boyfriend who can match your long-term goals.

It's entirely up to you and what you are looking for long-term and if you do have goals and ambitions in mind, then it may be helpful to date a guy who is willing to get up off the sofa and help you achieve those.

RED FLAG 9: You're an option not a priority

Have you ever dated someone who calls you at the last minute asking to meet? Spontaneity once in a while can be enjoyable, however if you feel you are regularly a last minute thought, then that's because you probably are.

The same applies if your date never considers you when making plans and chooses their friends over you. If you find yourself in this situation more than once, then I'm afraid to say you are an option not a priority.

If you think for one minute the relationship is off balance and only on their terms, then you need to do yourself a favour and stop seeing this time waster. You are worth more than an afterthought.

If you're sitting wondering, wait, am I his priority? Ask yourself the following questions: Does he give you notice for dates? Does he plan nice things to do together? If yes, then he's likely making you his priority. Woohoo! However if he is cancelling important plans you've invited him to or he won't skip a trip to the pub to be your date for a wedding, then you are not at the forefront of his mind.

Stop holding on to someone who treats you like an option and go find someone who makes you their priority.

RED FLAG 10: He drinks heavily/takes drugs/gambles

Whether you partake in gambling, recreational drugs, drink alcohol or not, it is wise that I advise you to stay away from someone who does to excess. What's excess? Well, that's up to you to decide. The bottom line is gambling, drugs and alcohol abuse is not only an illness, it's a relationship timebomb waiting to go off.

Addictions destroy relationships and ruin lives. It's a heart-breaking situation for everyone involved and I wouldn't wish addiction on my worst enemy.

For some women, the thought of dating a man who drinks a drop of alcohol, takes drugs or gambles, fills them with dread. For others, sharing a bottle of wine every night, placing bets daily or doing a line of coke on a Saturday night with their boyfriend is a way of bonding. Ultimately it is up to you to decide what you feel comfortable with.

If you think the man you are dating has an addiction, express your concerns. They may confess or deny that they have a problem. Whatever you do, protect yourself. This is a life-long illness that will no doubt cause you heartache in the long run.

I also want to make it clear that if you are dating an addict, you must never feel pressure to stay with them. It can be an incredibly exhausting experience, especially if he doesn't want to get help. If you are or know someone who is dealing with an addiction, I have placed some useful resources at the back of this book. Alternatively you can contact your GP or a mental health professional who will support you through this process.

RED FLAG 11: He breaks the law

It may not come as a surprise to you that anyone who breaks the law, would be categorised as a red flag, but unfortunately some women do choose to turn a blind eye to illegal behaviour. This is never a good idea, as criminal activity shouldn't be overlooked. Like ever. Whether that's dating a drug dealer or someone who regularly drives under the influence, these are some red flag signs that you shouldn't ignore.

Not only is breaking the law immoral, a study found that those who break the law are more likely to be narcissistic than those who don't commit crime. This is because narcissists act entitled and don't believe rules or the law apply to them.

Of course, not everyone who runs a red light or speeds is a psychopath. However if you're compliant like the vast majority, **I'd suggest avoiding irresponsible men who break the law. As they will no doubt break their promises and your heart too!**

CHAPTER 2 - DATING APPS

We live in a world where we can connect with people all over the globe, thanks to the beauty of technology. Which is all very impressive, but has made dating into a fucking minefield. It's true that online dating opened the door to endless possibilities and has been the reason for many happy marriages, but they've also caused plenty of problems. Firstly there is too much choice when it comes to people. Making us all feel like a kid in a candy store. There's a sense that there are infinite options for any of us, and that if we pick one we might be missing out on another.

All of that said, apps are the main way that people meet romantic partners in the 2020s, so they're an unavoidable fact of life. Rather than refusing to use them and potentially missing out on someone amazing, learn to use them in a smart way. And by smart, obviously I mean by learning to recognise red flags before you've wasted an evening sharing a bottle of wine at a mediocre pub.

RED FLAG 12: His profile has little information about him

Chances are the majority of men online won't have the best photos of themselves let alone enough information about them. I can't point to a study which explains why, but it's a pretty universal truth that men are terrible at picking photographs for their dating profiles. Which means that what they write about themselves is extra important. Anyone who just writes 'ask me' or 'get in touch' has made absolutely no effort in their profile, and will probably make similarly little effort with you.

If you find a profile you think might be interesting, but that's light on pictures or information, it's totally OK to ask for more details. Asking for their social media profile or more photos is acceptable dating app etiquette. On that note, be wary of those that don't provide you with more photos or a social media handle. This could mean that they are a catfish or in a relationship. Trust me, it happens. While it may seem dramatic, this is the internet after all, and there are a lot of weird and dangerous humans out there.

Protect yourself and ask as many questions as possible to help give you an indication if this match is a good or bad guy. Don't worry if you're coming across as an interrogator, if your match is a good guy, he should be pleased that you're taking an interest and asking for more information. There's no rush to go from chatting to meeting, so if you're not sure about someone, allow yourself some time to get to know each other before you commit to anything IRL.

If for whatever reason they refuse to give you more information or make you feel unreasonable for asking, then you need to swipe to the next man.

RED FLAG 13: His selfies are topless

There's quite a short list of photos that men post on their profiles. You will no doubt find that there are men who like to post smiley selfies or pics with their dog, or someone else's baby*. You'll also discover there will be men who love a topless selfie, flexing their muscles in the mirror or on the beach. If this is a look you're into, then please be my guest and swipe right.

In my experience, men who love nothing more than taking topless selfies are likely to take hours getting ready, stare at themselves in every mirror they walk by or live in the gym.

Of course, not everyone who posts a pouty or shirtless photo is a red flag. It's worth noting that it is totally acceptable when a man likes to take care of himself and show it off. If he's a model or personal trainer then I can understand the need for full body shots. However, it is sensible to weigh up how many topless selfies he has on his dating profile. If all of them are topless and pouting and he's allegedly a professional trader, then RUN SIS!

*Check that it is someone else's baby. It's amazing how many men don't feel the need to mention that they have children.

RED FLAG 14: The 'must haves' profile

Another red flag culprit you will discover on dating apps is the "must have" individual. This is when a man lists everything that he is looking for in a woman. For example, *said in sarcastic voice*:

She must be blonde
Must have no kids
Must be a virgin or only dated one man in her entire life
Must be gorgeous with a petite body and big boobs

Well, well, well. This is certainly a man who knows what he wants. I can tell you now, that even if you did tick all of his must haves, this man will still not be happy. For anyone thinking, 'Hang on, I wrote a list of don'ts and wants in a partner earlier, what's wrong with his list?'. Well to start, your list was private. You're not advertising it on a dating app and suggesting that anyone who doesn't meet it is some kind of failure.

The issue with the kind of list written above is that there is a fine line between deal breakers and being an arsehole. Men who are obsessed with a very specific body type or a woman's sexual history are, generally speaking, bad vibes.

On the flipside, if you stumble across a profile where someone states what they are looking for, is like this: 'Looking for someone who loves fitness as much as me but also enjoys eating pizza and beer', then I would say that person sounds realistic. These are reasonable preferences. It's the demanding and rigid men with sexist obsessions that you need to watch out for.

Those with an unrealistic 'must have' list, are likely to be delusional or worse controlling.

RED FLAG 15: He seems too good to be true

If he seems too good to be true...he probably is!

So let me paint the picture, you've matched with a guy and you're hitting it off. You share similar interests and you're telling each other stories that you wouldn't usually share. You feel comfortable because you both seem so alike, and he *seems* perfect.

News flash: no one is perfect.

Behind a phone screen, we can all pretend to be someone different. We have creative license to say all the things that will impress a stranger. That's the problem when meeting someone online: you don't know who they are.

There will be plenty of people who tell the truth online. Maybe they do have a holiday home in Spain and do lots of charity work for children. I would recommend that before you fall head over heels in love, that you do not get carried away with the initial hype. **Falling in love with the idea of someone before knowing them is a recipe for disaster.**

Don't rush and use these coming months as a trial to see if he really is who he says he is. This way you're protecting your heart, and hopefully saving yourself pain.

For those of us who were raised on a diet of too much Disney, it's tempting to believe that finally a knight in shining armour has come to save them. Ladies, we don't need a man to save us. **Keep in mind that the Knight in shining armour is probably just some twat wrapped in tin foil.**

RED FLAG 16: He's suggestive

You match with a man, who sends the following message to you:

Hi sexy *heart eyes emoji* Couldn't help but drool over your selfies. Love the one of you in that green

dress. Cute bum. You are the most beautiful
woman I've ever seen. Send me some more photos
or shall we video call I'd love to see your face?

Listen, I am all for compliments but when a guy only
compliments you for your physical attributes this is
probably because he thinks your appearance is the
most important thing about you. And it quite
possibly means that he only wants to sleep with
you.

While some of you may like this flirty tone, this
message is an obvious red flag because A) he is
calling you a pet name when he doesn't know you
B) he is clearly being suggestive when he doesn't
know you and C) he's not asking you questions to
get to know you. He just wants to see your face.

There's a fine line between flattery and coming
across as disrespectful. He may think you are the
most beautiful thing he's ever seen but focusing on
your looks and not asking questions about you is a
red flag. For all he knows you could be a psychotic
bunny boiler.

A woman with high self-esteem will have no desire
for validation like this and will see him for what he
is. This guy is a player and quite possibly a creep.
**Be smart when you meet someone online who
pays you too many compliments or is
suggestive. This man isn't looking for a serious**

relationship, he is looking to see if you don't have any standards.

RED FLAG 17: He takes a long time to message

We are all busy and life can get in the way most of the time, but **the truth is we are never too busy to do the things that we want to do.** When a man is terrible at replying or continually ghosts you and then reappears, this is a red flag. When communication is hot and cold, it's not only disheartening, it's a sign of disrespect.

There could be a number of reasons as to why men go AWOL, however it's not even worth wasting your energy on wondering why. If you find he takes too long to reply or isn't making the effort to progress your conversation, then he is probably not that interested.

Having said that, if your man is taking a few hours to reply, he is probably driving or busy at work, but if it's days at a time, then he's mugging you off.

Don't spend your life waiting for someone to message you. It's wasted effort and will only affect your confidence. Never take things personally either. If anything, be thankful that this man is showing you that you're not his priority.

RED FLAG 18: He's too keen to meet you

So you've just matched with this dude and you both send a couple of messages introducing yourselves. So far so good. Then he suggests taking things offline and meeting up for a drink. No big deal you might think. After all, isn't that the whole point of dating apps, to meet IRL?

Let's just focus on the situation for a second. **When an online match is eager to meet after only sending a couple of messages, you have to weigh up the possibilities as to why.** Sure you're funny and beautiful but this guy doesn't know enough about you. For all he knows you could be a murderer. Not to mention, you could be totally incompatible. While this could be possible with any online date, you run the risk of meeting a red flag when you know nothing about them.

Even if this man looks like a Greek Adonis, do not agree to meet. Suggest that you both get to know each other over the phone first. Once you have done your due diligence then you can take him up on his invitation. Just make sure you meet in a public place and not their home!

RED FLAG 19: He's too hesitant to meet you

An indecision is a decision.

If he's hesitant to meet you or hasn't asked you out on a date after days of talking, then this is a red flag. Even more so, if he's resistant to your suggestion that you take things offline.

While some people can be shy to make the first move, I would be cautious of anyone who doesn't suggest meeting or keeps putting it off. Whether he's shy, busy, in another relationship, a catfish or just wants you as a pen pal, I would stop investing energy into this man.

If he can't bring himself to organise a date or say yes to your suggestion of a date, there is a reason. And trust me, you don't want to waste your time hanging around to find out what that reason is.

RED FLAG 20: He keeps his dating profile active...even after making it exclusive with you

Let's say you meet someone online and everything has been going well. You have been getting to know each other over the last few months and you really like them. You talk to him every day and you have a good feeling that he could *finally* be the one. Until one day, your friend sends you a screenshot of a dating profile, asking: 'Hey, isn't this the guy you're dating?'. Yep. That's *your* man. His profile is still clearly active and he's even uploaded new photos. WTF!

What's worse, is he confirmed last month that he wanted you and him to be exclusive. However judging from his actions, what he probably meant by that is he wanted you to come off the market, while he plays the field.

While you may want to give this red flag the benefit of the doubt, I can assure you it won't be worth your time. He'll only make excuses like 'Oh, I forgot to delete it'. His dating profile (with newly uploaded photos) is still active because he is active.

If you've agreed to be exclusive, and the man you're seeing is still on dating apps, block and delete him, and never look back. This man is keeping his options open and I advise that you do the same.

CHAPTER 3 - THE FIRST DATE

Anyone can be charming for an evening. It's whether they are still wonderful months down the line that matters.

When it comes to first dates, it's a good idea to treat the situation casually. I sound like a broken record but this is the first stage of getting to know someone, so ask them lots of questions to determine if they tick any of your green or red flag boxes. Be careful to not act like you're in a job interview. You don't want to come across formal so make sure you keep the conversation flowing and occasionally ask open-ended questions that will give you an idea of who they are. "You mentioned visiting Sri Lanka, do you have plans to travel again soon?".

A lot of women can lose sight of their dealbreakers on a first date, especially if the man is dreamy and charming. That's when they are likely to get caught up in the romance of it all. It's vital that you keep your wits about you at all times, no matter how much you think you like your date. **Red flags can be very good at masking their real selves when you first meet them. Pay attention to their behaviour and don't turn a blind eye.**

The most important piece of advice when it comes to first dates, is no matter what happens, make sure you are yourself at all times. You may want to impress your date or change your opinions to accommodate them but this is just counterproductive. The idea of a first date is to work out whether you are equally matched or not, so be yourself.

Don't be afraid to tell your date that you are looking for a relationship. **There is nothing wrong with showing your cards early on a first date. If telling him what you are looking for scares him off, then good. He wasn't meant for you, and you've saved yourself some time**. That said, be careful to not overshare. **Confiding or oversharing with a potential red flag, is like giving them a manual on how to manipulate you.** So keep your childhood trauma or bowel movements to yourself or at least until you're in a serious and committed relationship.

If you can recognise a red flag from the moment you meet them, then you will be winning. However don't be disheartened if you keep spotting red flags a little later in your relationship. As I said earlier, some red flags can hide themselves very well. However I trust that this chapter will make you become hypersensitive to red flags during your first date.

RED FLAG 21: He's late to your date...and doesn't tell you

You agree to both meet at 7pm. You turn up at 7:05, only to discover he's not arrived yet. OK, that's fine. You take a seat and order yourself a glass of wine. You check your phone to see if he's been in touch. No messages and it's fifteen minutes into the date. Strange. You wait it out a little longer, checking your texts to make sure you've got the right venue and time. You're in the right place and the right time, so where is he?

Before you know it, 30 minutes have passed and he still hasn't messaged. Just as you're about to text to ask if he's ok, your date rocks up. He gives you a kiss 'hello' and says a mere apology for being late.

Regardless of this being a first date or not, being late is rude. **Sure, everyone can run late but without informing you beforehand or apologising after, is a big red flag.** This lame behaviour signals that he's disrespectful and has bad manners. Qualities I don't think you want in a boyfriend.

When a man shows up late this is his way of saying, 'I don't value your time'. How insulting is that? If this ever happens to you, you have every right to leave the date before he shows up. Feel free to tell him that timekeeping is very important to you and that you hope he won't make the same mistake for his next date. (Spoiler alert: he will).

It's up to you how late you're willing to allow someone to be, but I would suggest that anything more than 20 minutes without a seriously good excuse says: 'I really don't give a shit'.

RED FLAG 22: He looks terrible

Let's say you're on a first date and the man in question turns up wearing a tracksuit with yesterday's lunch stain on the front. Unless you don't care about being presentable, I would question why this man hasn't made the effort for you. He could have at least put on a clean jumper. As the waiter takes your order, you notice his hands are dirty and he smells as if he hasn't showered for days.

Perhaps his hands are dirty because he has been gardening all day or maybe his washing machine is broken and he can't wash his clothes? Or maybe the reason why he smells bad is because he's come straight from the gym? Unless he has a valid excuse for his lack of hygiene, there really is no excuse to not make an effort.

When it comes to being presentable, it demonstrates someone that takes care of themselves. When someone lacks good hygiene, I would also bet my last pound that their house will be incredibly dirty too. You may or may not have an

OCD, but personal hygiene should be important to you.

When someone turns up to a first date looking a mess, you have to ask yourself the question: why didn't he feel it was necessary to make the effort for me? Especially if you just bought a new outfit and spent hours on your hair.

If this guy can't make the effort for you now, he's not going to make the effort for you, ever.

RED FLAG 23: He's rude to waiters

You're on a first date and the conversation is flowing well. You're enjoying his company and he seems like a nice guy, that is until he signals for the waiter to come over by clicking his fingers. Wait what? Did he just click his fingers? The waiter comes over and your date talks to them as if they are incompetent and beneath them. The waiter looks at you and you look at the waiter. Surely this guy is not serious?

If your date is rude to waiters or anyone for that matter, then you can be certain this person is either nasty or an over-privileged idiot. If you see anyone behave in this way, call them out. Then exit the venue and block this guy's number.

RED FLAG 24: He isn't present

Imagine this: you're on a first date and during your conversation, your date keeps checking his phone. To add insult to injury every time you talk, he can't give you eye contact as he's too busy looking around the room or over your shoulder.

There is nothing more frustrating and demeaning when someone isn't present. This behaviour is a red flag because this man isn't actively trying to get to know you and is openly demonstrating his lack of interest in you. It's bad manners.

Similarly, if he's not asking you questions about yourself, or he's giving you the shortest possible answers to your questions, that's really not a good sign.

Whether this is your first date or ten-year anniversary, you want to feel that your partner is paying attention to you. **If he is more distracted by his phone or other people in the room, then this is a clear sign that he's not interested in you.**

If you ever find yourself in this situation, take this as your cue to ask for the bill and get the hell out of there.

RED FLAG 25: He love bombs you

'Love bombing' is a manipulation tactic that red flags use when trying to make you fall in love with them, so they can abuse you later down the line. You can usually spot love bombing, as it comes in the form of excessive affection, gifts and compliments all within the first couple of months of dating. Of course, it's normal to like receiving gifts or compliments, or wanting to feel special every now and again, but when someone goes overboard in the initial stages of dating, this is a red flag.

While some people are naturally kind, you have to be wary of people's intentions. So how can you tell the difference between love bombing and genuine love? Love bombers rush the natural process of the relationship, whereas a healthy relationship takes time to build. Love bombing tends to happen in the initial stages of dating, so keep that in mind when someone proclaims their undying love for you or asks for exclusivity or calls you their 'soulmate', when you've only known them for less than five minutes. While there are a few real-life cases of "love at first sight" that are totally legit - if we're being honest with ourselves, those are few and far between.

It can be tempting to believe in your own hype, but it's important you keep your barriers up when getting to know someone. Love bombers can easily fool people into a false sense of security which will allow them to abuse and control you at a later stage. **So be cautious of compliments and gifts, as they could come with a sinister cost.**

RED FLAG 26: He's derogatory

A bit of flirtation and teasing during the first date is a good way to bond with each other. But if your date makes comments that are mean, or that you find offensive, do not ignore. You are not being too sensitive.

If he makes a dig about what you're wearing or tells you that you're not smart enough to understand what he is talking about, it's probably not flirty banter. It's almost certainly a red flag. It might not feel like a big deal at that moment in time, but imagine it happening day after day, week after week. Eventually it will destroy your self-esteem. If you're not sure whether he's crossing the line, try responding honestly. If you say 'That's not funny – please don't speak to me like that' and he's apologetic and then stops, that's one thing. But if he tells you that you 'can't take a joke' or becomes defensive? Big fat red flag.

It's critical that you are wary of men who tease, pay back-handed compliments or mansplain. Any man who insults or makes derogatory comments is likely to be emotionally abusive and controlling in the future. Let alone disrespectful.

More often than not, when a man is derogatory it's usually because he feels insecure around you and wants to take you down a peg or two. This is also called 'Negging'. Negging is an act of emotional manipulation, whereby a person makes a deliberate backhanded compliment or insult, to undermine someone's confidence and increase their need for the negger's approval. Sometimes disguised as constructive criticism or questions that are actually insults, for example: "Don't take this wrong but as your dress is already tight, do you really want to eat that?".

Similarly, if he talks about other women in a derogatory fashion in an attempt to build you up, for example, saying things like 'You're not like other girls – they're all so obsessed with getting likes on Instagram.'. Run a mile. He doesn't like women, and while he might fancy you, eventually it'll become clear that deep down he doesn't like you either.

Don't accept any rude comments, even if he claims 'it's just a joke'. If you are insulted, hurt or upset, then grab your coat and ask him to settle the bill. **Go and find yourself a man who builds you up, not brings you down to his level.**

RED FLAG 27: He's sarcastic and makes too many jokes

It's usually a good sign when someone makes you laugh or has a similar sense of humour to you. Joking and playing around is also a great way to break the ice on a first date, but if you find your date is making joke after joke and refusing to interact on any serious points, this could be an indication that he is a man-child or fearful of intimacy.

Making continuous jokes could be a sign they are nervous but it can also be a sign they are avoiding you from getting too close. On the other hand, if your date is sarcastic and doesn't take anything you say seriously, then it's likely he doesn't respect you.

Having a good sense of humour is great, but you're looking for a relationship, not a front row seat to his comedy show. If this guy continues his lame routine of jokes, rather than listen or take you seriously, I'd wave goodbye to this clown and leave him at the circus.

The last thing you want is to end up in a relationship that becomes the ultimate joke.

FLAG 28: He admits he doesn't want a girlfriend

If you're sitting opposite your first date and he tells you that he isn't looking for a girlfriend right now. Believe him.

By putting all his cards on the table and not hiding his lack of commitment is a great exit-opener for you. If for whatever reason you just want to have fun and no strings attached with this guy, then go for it. Because that's all you will ever have.

For those who are looking for a relationship, do not take it personally when someone tells you they are not looking for commitment. Think of it this way, this guy is doing you a huge favour by being honest. So instead of getting caught up in thinking you can change his mind, let him go.

He will not be convinced that he really does want a girlfriend if he just gets to know you. He has been honest with you. Respect that.

Do not waste your time by seeing this guy again, just accept the fact that this man's needs do not match your own. Be thankful that he's been so transparent and move on.

RED FLAG 29: He says: "Your place or mine?"

You've finished dinner and the first date has gone exceptionally well. That is until he tries to convince you to go back to his or your place for a night cap. As tempting as this might be when we like someone, it's best to call it a night and arrange another date.

There is a good reason for doing this. 1) You are simply setting boundaries and standards for yourself. 2) It will be a good test to see if he respects your decision or if he tries to push you into coming home with him/you.

The right man will respect you, the wrong man will try and pressure you. **Any man who pushes you into anything is a red flag and should be left well alone.**

FLAG 30: He doesn't make plans to see you again

Your first date went really well and you assume a second date will happen. Only that it's been a couple of days and he still hasn't contacted you or replied to your message.

Hate to break it to you but unless this guy has lost his phone or fallen down a hole, he is probably not that into you.

It's not rocket science, when someone is interested, they will contact you within a few days and make plans to see you again.

Some women will tell themselves that this particular man is too shy or 'useless' at initiating or maintaining contact. Sure, we could all make excuses – maybe he lost his phone or got hit by a car or he's been deported. But realistically, as the old expression goes, if he's not making plans with you then he's just not that into you.

If he likes you, he will contact you. If he doesn't then treat this man like he's dead and let him rest in peace.

CHAPTER 4 - SOCIAL MEDIA

For many of us social media has become a part of our everyday lives. It has changed the way we communicate and connect with people and it has given us a platform to express ourselves in the form of videos, photos and words.

Social media has done a lot of good but what has it done to dating and relationships?

Social scientists already know there's a link between social media use and mental health disorders, such as depression, anxiety, and low self-esteem. Unsurprisingly, researchers have also found a connection between social media and break-ups.

Social media has caused angst in the dating world because of the never-ending problems it brings. It has been the cause for many people to stray because of it's open access to anyone we want. And I'm in no doubt that social media has been the cause of many arguments amongst couples - whether it's a "like" on someone's photo or sending flirty messages to other people. Then add the societal pressure of social media on top of that, with people posting never-ending photos of how 'perfect' their life and relationship is. This comparison of his vs her life can make even the most secure individuals insecure.

Yup, social media has made dating tricky. However the great thing about social media is it can give you a rough idea as to whether your date is worth pursuing. While the majority of us only share the good parts of our world, social media can also show the negative. If you look closely...

RED FLAG 31: He's always online

Unless the man you are dating is a celebrity, influencer or owns an online business, I would err with caution as to why he is constantly online. And even then, work/life balance is important, and it's rude to be on your phone when you're supposed to be on a date or hanging out with someone.

Firstly, why does he need to broadcast his life or engage with others constantly? Is it to connect with people or is the need for validation?

Secondly, does he work in the media and has to use social media, 24/7 for his job? If not, then could his obsession simply be down to immaturity and not living life offline?

Thirdly, is he addicted to social media? Social media addiction is very real and can cause a lot of problems for people and those around them.

Lots of us rack up more weekly screen time than we should, but if he's genuinely incapable of putting his phone down and focusing on his time with you, that's a really terrible sign.

If the guy you are seeing is constantly online, then I'd do yourself a favour and 'log off'.

RED FLAG 32: He follows a lot of bikini models and Only Fans girls

Social media gives us access to many things. We can find someone and gain an insight into their life within a matter of seconds. While you can tell a lot about someone from their photos and the locations they spend most of their time at; **you can also tell a lot about a man by who he follows on social media.**

Is he following thousands of naked women and models? Is he following racist or homophobic pages? Is he following weird cults and conspiracy groups? If he is, then you need to unfollow him right now.

If he's following lots of naked women, you can take that as a sign he's been around the block a few times. If the women are Only Fans girls, models or porn stars, you can either brand him as a sleaze or immature. Unless these are women who he is friends with in real life, or women who post a mixture of content, it's not a great sign.

People often forget that you can see what posts they've liked online. Taking a quick look at everything he's liked on Twitter or Instagram is a fantastic insight into their psyche.

As for the racist and homophobic pages, you shouldn't go anywhere near this man if he is supporting discrimination or hate. It's never 'just a joke'.

I think it's always a good idea for any woman to do her due diligence before she 'yes' to a date. And the best and easy way to do that, is to check his social media and who he follows.

RED FLAG 33: The same women like and comment on his posts every time

Want to know if the man you've set your sights on is a player or has a girlfriend? Take a look at his recent five posts. If the same woman (or women) comment with heart eye emojis or like his posts, then you have possibly found a man who has a girl, or more on the scene.

Sure, the women in question may be just friends but take this as a light warning that you could be entering red flag territory.

If you have been dating for some time (read: months), I would ask who these women are. Some men may try to pull out the 'she's just a friend' card, so if he does this (and you haven't met her), I'd suggest that you all meet up for a drink, so he can introduce you to his 'friend'. Anyone he has an innocent relationship with will be fair game for group socialisation – and it's nice to have a chance to bond with the people he cares about.

If for whatever reason you are feeling insecure or uncomfortable about who he follows, then you need to speak up and tell him. Don't worry about coming across as jealous. As long as you address the concern in a calm way, he should be respectful and responsive to your concerns.

RED FLAG 34: He doesn't follow you or interact with your posts

While many of these red flags are to do with the other person, there are some issues that you can relax on. For example, when dating a man who won't follow you on social media, don't be alarmed. Simply ask him why.

He may be a private person who prefers to not see the person he is dating online. After all, social media can cause arguments. If that's the case, then you need to respect his decision. However if he is constantly watching your stories or visiting your profile, then you can raise the red flag on this one.

Does he have a girlfriend/wife who would start asking questions? Or is he hiding a second life on his private account?

The same goes for accepting photo tags. If he is removing the tags you're tagging him in, then I would see this as a sign of him caring what others think or that he doesn't want to be seen with you. As I always say, trust your gut. Ask him why he doesn't accept requests or tags and see what he says.

If his reason isn't convincing or you feel a pang of dishonesty, then get the hell out of there.

RED FLAG 35: His DM replies are flirty

Sliding into someone's DMs is not a problem when a man is single, but if he's dating you and sending flirty messages to other women, then this is disrespectful.

If he is messaging other women in a flirtatious manner or reacting to someone's story with a love heart emoji, then this indicates that this man is a player. It's tempting to write it off as 'just an online thing', but don't. This is the type of behaviour from a man, you shouldn't trust. **If he's craving validation online, he is likely to seek it offline.**

RED FLAG 36: He airs his dirty laundry and fights online

There is nothing worse than going online and reading someone's Facebook status on how much they hate so-and-so or how shit their day has been. But just imagine if that person was someone you were dating.

#cringe

Social media is all about sharing however there are some things that should be left behind closed doors. When a man airs his dirty laundry online, this is a red flag because it shows he can't stop his mouth (or fingers) from running wild.

If he's aggressive towards people online, he might well be aggressive in real life, and we all know that's not a good sign.

Even sharing too much information about you and your relationship, is still a cause for concern. If he broadcasts everything that you do together, he is probably going to announce your break-up too.

And if he's an internet troll, then you need to get away ASAP! When a man overshares on the internet, it shows immaturity and a need for validation. Unfollow this keyboard warrior and find a man who maintains a bit of mystery.

RED FLAG 37: He doesn't post you on his social media after months of dating

Social media isn't real life and it's important to not get caught up in the over exposure culture that we've developed as a society.

Not every man likes using social media. If he never posts photos of his life, then it is unlikely he will post a photo of you both. However, if he is an avid user and he can't even post you in his story or be tagged in a photo with you, then this is a red flag.

Ask him what his reasons are for keeping the relationship private online. It could be that he wants to keep it that way and that he doesn't want to publicise your romance. This is a fair excuse and you should respect this. However if your gut instinct is screaming that there's another reason for his discreet behaviour, I'd investigate as to why you think that. Has he not taken other steps to show his commitment? Is he shady with his phone?

Weigh up whether you think this guy is here for the long haul or is keeping you hidden until someone else comes along.

RED FLAG 38: You stalk him online

Now the tables have turned. I've placed the red flag onto your behaviour, because stalking the person you are dating online usually indicates that *you* don't trust him.

Trust is the key to all relationships and if there isn't any trust, then you have nothing. Maybe you don't trust him because you saw something suspicious on his phone or maybe your gut is burning inside because you know there is something not right about this guy.

Do not waste hours or days, trying to find something on his social media profile that might fuel or confirm your lack of trust. If you're not trusting him offline, then you need to end this relationship.

CHAPTER 5 - COMMUNICATION

It's no secret that good communication is the key to having a happy and successful relationship. Communication at its core, whether verbal, written or physical, is all about connecting and understanding one another.

When it comes to dating, if you and your partner have established a healthy space for you both to convey your point of view, along with showing support and understanding for each other, then you stand a good chance of going the distance.

On the flip side, poor communication is a relationship killer. Many of you will no doubt know that miscommunication can be incredibly frustrating and exhausting. Whether it's your partner not listening and understanding your needs, or your partner ignoring you, this is when intimacy breaks down.

In a nutshell, to form a good rapport of communication, you and your partner have to be open and honest. Communication is a two-way street and something that constantly needs to be worked on. If you find that the guy you are dating cannot communicate effectively, then this is likely to cause you more problems than good.

RED FLAG 39: He says "I love you" too soon

So it's been a couple of months now (read: anywhere from 1 day to 6 months) and you've been dating this great guy. All is going well, until he blurts out over dinner, that he loves you.

Here's the thing, when a man says, 'I know this is crazy, as I haven't known you for that long...but I love you'. He's right, that is crazy!

While it's a nice thought to believe someone instantly fell in love with you, it's very important to remind yourself that in the early days, months, even one year of dating, you are still getting to know someone. Mark Twain said that "Love seems the swiftest, but it is the slowest of all growths. No man or woman really knows what perfect love is until they have been married a quarter of a century.". Twain makes a good point.

Of course, I am in no doubt that you are a fabulous and wonderful person, and who wouldn't love you within months of knowing you? But when a man hasn't taken the time to get to know you and rushes to say the 'L' word, that should ring 'Love bombing' alarm bells.

It's very common for a manipulative or controlling man to 'love bomb' in the early days of dating as it can lull women into a false sense of security. Early love confessions can also be a sign of immaturity or just plain bullshit. Don't fall for it.

Love takes time to build and while we can all feel loved-up at the start of a relationship, we must remember that these feelings are often lust and not love. A 2017 study in the *Personal Relationships journal* orchestrated a bunch of first encounters between single strangers, and the researchers found feelings of instant attraction can indeed happen in a first encounter. Some people described these feelings as "love at first sight" however, these people didn't report feelings of intimacy, passion, and commitment as part of their experience.

So what's a girl to do when a man throws a love bomb in the early stages? Pull back. Keep this man at arm's length. Watch how he reacts to this. Does he immediately get angry or ghost you? If so, this man is a red flag. Kick him to the curb.

If he claims he was just drunk and he's terribly sorry, then if you want to, you can give this immature buffoon the benefit of the doubt. (though personally, I wouldn't bother).

If he is adamant that he loves you, listen to your intuition. Have there been other red flags? A sign of a good and healthy partner is a man who can control his emotions and knows the importance of getting to know you first, before telling you he loves you.

RED FLAG 40: He texts too much

For many millennials and Gen Z, texting is a major source of relationship communication. It's how we flirt, check-in, ask questions, gossip, make plans or otherwise connect with potential or current romantic partners.

Texting is great but then texting can be less useful if the person we're dating doesn't stop messaging. Take my friend's example below. This is a message from a guy she had been dating for over a month. Although she is no longer dating him...and you will see why:

9:05am
Good morning beautiful. Hope your day goes well. Xx

10:34am
Morning!
I am so so busy - work is crazy today. Not gonna be on my phone much. Hope your day is good :) x

11:35am
Hey
Want to grab lunch at 1? xx

12:50pm
?

12:51pm

??

13:15pm
Hey, sorry I can't today. Like I said this morning, I'm really busy with work.

13:15pm
Ha ha thought you ghosted me.

13:38pm
Fancy getting a coffee this afternoon?

13:50pm
I have tickets to a gig tomorrow, do you want to come with me?

13:53pm
What you up to? x

Constant and impatient texts like the example above, is a big red flag when it comes to the early stages of dating. Not only does constant texting show insecurity, it can be a sign of disrespect, especially if they keep bombarding you even after you've communicated your texting boundaries (I can't talk right now/I'm having a digital detox/I don't use my phone during work hours etc). If you communicate clearly and he doesn't take the information in, he's clearly not listening to you or simply doesn't care.

Pay attention to how he reacts when you communicate your texting T&Cs. If they continue to message you throughout the day and accuse you of neglecting or ignoring them, then you will need to take a large step back. This is not only suffocating behaviour, this is bordering on controlling.

RED FLAG 41: He rarely texts and never calls you back (but is always on his phone)

If it takes a guy days to respond to your texts or he never calls you back, then you are not his priority.

This man has clearly got something else going on in his life or someone else in the pipeline. If he liked you, he would find the time to text or call. **No matter how busy our schedule, we can always find time for the things that we want to do.** Of course, if he's at work, a family event or has boundaries as to when he uses his phone, then this is totally acceptable and you should respect this. But if he's playing on his phone and ignoring you, then this is a dick move.

Nowadays we're all glued to our phone, so if the man you're dating isn't making time to message you, then you need to reclaim your time and go elsewhere.

You deserve a man who wants to hear your voice at the end of a busy day or will send you a funny meme to make you laugh. Oh and please don't believe any of his excuses like, "I'm just bad at texting". This is a lame excuse teenagers invented in the early 00's.

RED FLAG 42: He doesn't listen to you

There is nothing worse than sharing details about your day or a funny story you've been dying to tell your man, only for him to not listen to a word you've said.

Let's face it, we all expect our partners to make the effort to listen to us. How else can we bond or convey how we feel? Listening is the key to effective communication and when someone doesn't listen it can make you feel unworthy, not to mention frustrated and unhappy.

Your significant other doesn't need to recall your conversations word for word, but if he never pays attention while you're talking, then this is a red flag.

Anyone who respects or cares for you, will make the time to listen and take a genuine interest in what you have to say. If they would rather talk exclusively about themselves, then this is a red flag that you are dating a selfish man who is incapable of being in a relationship. Or worse a narcissist.

Interestingly, when you leave this relationship, these are the types of red flags that will start to listen to you as you walk out of the door. Just keep walking and don't bother sticking around to 'listen' to their excuse. You shouldn't need to leave for your partner to hear what you're saying. Similarly, if he only takes your feelings seriously when you're upset, that's a red flag.

RED FLAG 43: He brings up your faults or past mistakes

The moment a man brings up your faults or past mistakes to purposefully make you feel bad, that's when it's time to say goodbye to this jerk.

While your partner has every right to ask you to acknowledge or discuss your bad behaviour, a person who constantly criticises you or who uses your faults or mistakes against you, is not a good person. **A good partner will bring up problematic behaviours in an attempt to move forward together, not use them as a stick to hit you with.**

If your man regularly hurts or puts you down, this is a red flag sign of abuse. Abusive men love to use their partner's bad habits, flaws or mistakes as a way to belittle and give them respite for *their* poor behaviour. This is a dangerous game and a game that you will never win.

If your man is keeping score, this is not love. This is a manipulative and abusive mind game, so don't let him play you. Leave.

RED FLAG 44: He never says sorry

Not accepting responsibility for poor behaviour is a major red flag.

Taking responsibility for our actions is not only an act of maturity, but also the key to maintaining a healthy relationship. If your man can't bring himself to put his hands up and apologise for his fuck-ups, then you are likely dating a man-child, master manipulator or a prick.

How he apologies is also incredibly important. A real apology means saying: 'I am sorry.' Not 'I am sorry but…' followed by a string of reasons why their behaviour was actually totally reasonable. Or 'I'm sorry that you chose to get offended' which places all the blame on you.

An inability to apologise or take accountability for their mistakes is a sign of disrespect. If you ever find yourself in a situation where the man you're dating won't acknowledge his portion of your shared problems, you need to do yourself a favour and tell him that *you* are sorry, but "I won't be pursuing this relationship any further".

An adult relationship is where both partners are willing to resolve issues through the power of saying 'sorry' and taking responsibility for their behaviour.

RED FLAG 45: He lies

While we can all tell a little white lie here and there, full blown lying is a recipe to sabotage any relationship.

A healthy relationship involves honesty and transparency. A relationship that consists of lying or is built on a foundation of lies, is most likely doomed to fail. How could you ever trust someone who can't be honest and tell the truth?

Men often excuse their lies as something they said to avoid you from getting hurt. While this can be excused for innocence or situational, when a lie is told for his own benefit and not yours, this cannot be excused. Who isn't to say that after one lie, he won't continue lying to you about bigger things further down the line? Don't believe me, read Hannah's* story:

'When I first met Sam*, he told me that he owned his own marketing consultancy and that he hadn't spoken to his ex in years.

'As the months rolled on, I soon learnt that he didn't own his business. His friend did. Sam was employed as a freelancer. I didn't take this lie to be that big of a deal and I brushed it off. I convinced myself that to be a freelancer you are technically self-employed, which means you are your own boss. I was naive.

'Then, six months into our relationship, I started discovering other things he had told me that weren't true. Stuff like he owned his house outright but he was actually only renting it. He always had an excuse for his lies and even though I claimed to believe it, deep down I would question it.

'When we were just about to celebrate our one-year anniversary, his ex contacted me out of the blue. The ex he had allegedly not spoken to in years. She told me they had been having an affair for months.

'It was at that moment I realised I had been dating a compulsive liar and I just knew I could never trust him again. One of my biggest regrets is not leaving from the very first moment I caught him lying.'

Like Hannah's story, when a man tells a lie once you will always question his truths. **Never overlook**

a lie. Little lies are likely to turn into bigger and darker ones over time.

RED FLAG 46: He isn't transparent

There is nothing more frustrating than a man who doesn't tell you how he feels. If a man can't express his vulnerabilities, opinions or thoughts to you then this is a bad sign.

You are not a mind reader, so if he isn't communicating with you, then your relationship cannot progress.

Another red flag is when a man isn't transparent with you about where he's been or who he's hanging out with. While everyone is entitled to their own privacy and freedom, if a man is consistently defensive about his behaviour then this is a sign that he is likely hiding something from you. Most likely another woman (or other women). Of course, you don't need to know his every move but dating an elusive man isn't a pleasant experience. It's this lack of communication and behaviour that will trigger your insecurities and make you feel like you're dating a secret agent.

So what happens when a guy can't be transparent with you? You make it crystal clear that this isn't the relationship you deserve or want. Wave him goodbye and don't look back!

RED FLAG 47: He only calls you at night or when he's drunk

When a guy only calls you at night or when he's drunk, he's not contacting you for a friendly catch-up. He's calling you because he wants you as his booty call.

While it may seem cute that he's thinking of you, if he's only sexting and drunk calling asking to come over, I would take a big bet that he's not looking for anything serious. Or has messaged twenty other girls in his phone book too.

This guy is clearly after one thing and one thing only, and that one thing is not a late night conversation about politics.

If you're only looking for sex and not a relationship, then skip this chapter. Just make sure you wear a condom. For anyone else who is looking for a relationship, stay away from men that only contact you at night or drunk. Why? Because a man who wants to settle down, calls you in the daytime and arranges a date (sober).

If you don't want to be a booty call, I suggest you turn your phone off at night and never speak to this horny fool again.

RED FLAG 48: He makes you feel like you're treading on eggshells

Whether you've been dating for a short while or been together for a year or more, if you can't communicate your feelings to the person you are dating, then you need to ask yourself why. Are you incapable of opening up or are you scared of how he'll react?

If you don't feel comfortable around your man when it comes to communicating, then this is a cause for concern. First you need to establish whether the problem is you or the man you are dating. If you feel like you're treading on eggshells around your man because of how he'll react, when you express your thoughts or feelings, then this is a red flag sign that you could be in an abusive relationship.

A healthy relationship consists of good communication where both parties can talk openly and honestly with each other. With the right person you should be able to communicate whatever is on your mind. **If you can't express yourself in someone's company, then it is likely you are in the wrong company.**

CHAPTER 5 - EXES

We all have a history. I have an ex, you have an ex and I'm certain all the people you will date will also have exes. For most people, an ex will become a person that they used to know and who no longer exists in their life. However some people remain good friends with their ex. This might be for logistical reasons like having children together or it could be because they still have affection for each other and want to remain friends.

Being friends with an ex is a controversial topic, but as far as I'm concerned, considering that many breakups are often filled with drama and discord, remaining on friendly terms with an ex can be a sign of maturity in your partner.

I appreciate that some women might feel threatened by the idea of their boyfriend being friends with an ex. But as long as your partner has healthy boundaries with this person, it's important to keep your jealousy under control.

That said, if you do have an instinct that your ex has unresolved feelings or that he is crossing boundaries, then this does need to be addressed.

Ultimately if you sense the guy you're dating is still friends with his ex because he can't let go of her romantically, rather than because they've developed their relationship into something platonic, that's a red flag.

In any relationship, you need to feel reassurance and to understand the reason(s) for the continuing friendship with their ex. Without that, there is guaranteed to be issues. No-one wants to be the 'it's her or me' girl, but anyone you're getting into a serious romantic relationship with should prioritise your comfort and make you feel not threatened by other women.

RED FLAG 49: He's not over his ex

"The best way to get over someone is to get under someone else".

Unsurprisingly this is the kind of advice that men really enjoy when they're trying to heal a heartbreak. If only 'go to therapy' was so popular.

The issue with this method of recovery is that he's effectively using you as an emotional dishcloth. As your new guy distracts himself from his heartbreak, you end up being the rebound and get hurt in the process.

It's no secret that it takes time to move on from a break-up and sadly there is no time schedule to how long feelings can last. Recovering from a heartache can take days, weeks, months or even years. It all depends on the person and their situation.

If your man's breakup happened recently, and he still seems to be hurting over it, then this is a red flag you need to stay away from. **Entering into a relationship with a man who is still thinking about someone else is enough of a reason to end things.**

RED FLAG 50: He talks about his ex all the time

You're on a first date and while chatting over dinner, he mentions his ex. You didn't even ask about her, and yet he tells you that she *loves* sushi. You shrug it off and change the subject but then he mentions her again. This time telling you about their travelling adventures together. *Lovely.* You proceed to move the conversation again, but he stops you as he wants to tell you about that time when he and her went to Italy. Oh, and did you know she plays tennis every Sunday? By the time it comes to dessert you know her full name, date of birth and blood type.

This man could be best friends with his ex or hate her with a passion, but if he is constantly talking about her, then it is likely he isn't over her. It's also not uncommon for men to talk about their past as a test to see how you will react. Either way this behaviour is a red flag. **When it comes to dating,**

you should never feel that you are competing with another woman. If you sense that you are, let the other woman have him.

Ex-talk is fine after you have dated for a while, and knowing the topline details about the relationship is healthy. However if he is bringing her up at any given minute – whether to praise or disparage her - this is a red flag hitting you straight in the face.

When a man refuses to leave his ex in the past, it is extremely likely that he is not over her or in the right headspace for a serious relationship. He is either looking for a rebound or company and this is not what you're here for.

RED FLAG 51: He refuses to talk about his ex, full stop

You know what's almost as bad as talking about your ex non-stop: refusing to talk about them at all.

We should all know by now (especially as we're deep into this book) that the hallmark of a healthy relationship is trust. If your man isn't honest about his past, then this is a red flag you shouldn't ignore.

I dated a guy who refused to tell me anything about his ex and why they broke up. At first I thought I may have been a little intrusive, so I backed off. But after a while, curiosity got the better of me and I approached the sore subject again. I sensed that something bad had happened. The truth is, something bad had happened. In fact something bad was happening. He was still dating her.

When a man is tight-lipped about why his relationship ended, it is usually a red flag sign that he is either hiding something or can't be open with you.

If it is the latter, give him time to open up and tell him that you are here to support him. If for whatever reason your partner still doesn't want to divulge (even with a gentle bit of encouragement) then be honest with him, and explain that you feel suspicious by his vagueness.

Of course, not everyone feels comfortable sharing every single detail of their life, but if he is secretive about why his relationship ended and defensive when the topic comes up, this could be your cue to leave. For all you know, he could have cheated or stolen money from her. Or like my case, still dating her.

RED FLAG 52: He compares you to his ex

Being constantly compared to someone else, let alone an ex-girlfriend, can feel demeaning.

When I was in an abusive relationship, my boyfriend would regularly compare me to his exes. My cooking was never as good as Sabrina's* and apparently, I also didn't have an even temper like her. Pitting people against each other is a very common manipulative tactic that abusers use to make their victims insecure.

When a man compares you to an ex, good or bad, this is usually a red flag sign that he's not over her or is trying to make you feel insecure by creating unnecessary competition. Whatever the reason, us girls need to remember that when a guy compares you to someone else, he is openly saying that he can't accept certain parts of you. Even if he compares you to his ex in a favourable way, "You're so much prettier than Sabrina", this shouldn't be a conversation that ever enters into your relationship. Why? Because your relationship should be focused on just you and him. Not him, you and her.

RED FLAG 53: He's friends with his ex

There's nothing inherently wrong with your man speaking to his ex. If he had an amicable split with his ex and they're still on good terms, that's a good sign. The fact that they can be friendly with one another and not hold any resentment should be an indication that he's a mature and reasonable human. However you need to be sure that the relationship has changed, not that he's still living in the past.

If your man still speaks to his ex on an emotional level and tells her things like 'I miss you' or meets up with her in secret, then that's because he has unfinished business with her.

My friend Kate* dated a guy who would secretly text his ex and meet up with her behind Kate's back. When she eventually found out and confronted him about the situation. He admitted that he was still emotionally invested and wasn't quite ready to let go. Classic!

At the end of the day, you can't stop someone from communicating with their ex. The only thing you can do is trust your gut instinct as to whether or not he still carries a torch for her. If you truly believe he has feelings for his ex then you need to end the relationship.

It takes two to tango not three. You are not a rebound. This guy has a lot of work to do on himself so let him work out his problems on his own, while you continue your quest to find the one. **Don't do a load of emotional labour to get him ready for his next girlfriend.**

RED FLAG 54: He says his ex is a psycho or crazy

Story as old as time: your new guy has just told you that his ex was crazy. Do you know what, maybe she was crazy. Crazily tired of all his bullshit.

We've heard it all before. His ex is a psycho and he had to dump her. While in some cases it may be true, however speaking ill of an ex, is usually a red flag. The biggest red flag is if he doesn't just speak ill of one ex – but of all of them. If every woman he has dated is a 'psycho' then you have to ask yourself: what do all these 'crazy' women have in common?

Most women think that by a man disliking a woman, it means he despises her, but this isn't entirely true. It can be a red flag that he isn't over her.

There are two sides to every story, so listen to how he speaks about his ex. Is it demeaning? Is it rude? If it is, don't be fooled into thinking he wouldn't talk about you like this one day.

CHAPTER 6 - SEX

One of my favourite self-help books is 'Why Men Love Bitches' by Sherry Argov. In it there is a line which says: *Before sex, a man isn't thinking clearly and a woman is thinking clearly. After sex, it reverses. The man is thinking clearly and a woman isn't.'.*

Not to go all scientific on you but there are studies that have found that after sex, women release the hormone oxytocin, which creates the desire for attachment. This means that when your partner isn't around to give you some nookie - you produce less oxytocin. As a result you will crave sex and that person more. Hence we can feel needy and want cuddles after a passionate affair. Men don't get the same oxytocin hit as women do, in fact, after sex men feel relieved and that's it.

With the difference of hormones being released and women feeling naturally more connected than men after sex. It might be worth keeping this in mind when it comes to matters of the heart.

That said, there are no rules to sex and dating. If you want to sleep with someone on the first date or months down the line - as long as it's consensual, you must do what feels right. However my only piece of advice is to use a condom! With sexual diseases on the rise, my number one rule before getting in between the sheets, is that you wear a condom. If the thought of rubber repulses the man in question or he refuses to wear one, take this as a big red flag sign that he is not a nice man. Don't waste your breath explaining sexual health or the risk of pregnancy to this idiot, just get your stuff and go.

So back to sex. Safe sex is great fun. Yet sadly some men can abuse this wonderful act for their own gain. Make sure that you keep your head above sexual waters and understand that sex isn't the gateway to commitment. It's the path to sex. If at any point, you feel that you are being used for sex or that the man you're dating isn't putting your needs first, you need to stop and reassess the situation. Do I feel comfortable with this situation? Is this man prioritising my feelings and safety over getting his dick wet? Is this consensual?

If at any point you feel you are being forced to have sex or perform a sexual act that you are not comfortable with, then this is serious alarm bells. A high quality man will never force or pressure you. They understand consent. And just to reiterate, consent is not just a once-off question (although the question is very important!). Consent is continuously checking in with the other person, every step of the way. That is where enthusiastic consent comes in. Enthusiastic consent is about ensuring that all parties are enthusiastically consenting to everything that happens during sex. This means you would be participating in sexual acts because you're excited about it, not because you feel pressured into it. Enthusiastic consent gives power to each individual to decide if they want to have sex and how they want to have it.

RED FLAG 55: Sex with you is more important than getting to know you

At the start of dating, you may find some men will want to have sex with you straight away. However this is no excuse for a man to push or rush you into any sexual activity.

While I know I sound like a broken record and repeating myself; when spending time with a man, observe how much effort he puts into wanting to get to know you. Is he putting in more effort to get you into bed? Or is he asking genuine questions about yourself?

It's worth adding here, that men will also say and do anything to get you into bed. So be careful of these red flags. **A man could ask you all the questions in the world and treat you like a princess, but once he's got what he wants. He leaves.**

Yes, dating is tiring. That's why we need to take our time when getting to know someone outside and inside the bedroom.

RED FLAG 56: He pressures you to have sex

Sexual coercion can be exerted in a number of ways, however it is totally unacceptable for someone to pressure you into any sexual activity.

'No' is not a challenge and if he keeps pursuing his desire to sleep with you, this is not because he's into you, it's because he disrespects you.

The same goes for your contraception preferences, if he doesn't want to wear a condom but you do. Then you need to tell him that your sexual health is non-negotiable. Don't lower your standards to appease a man. If he continues to apply pressure or even sneakily tries to remove the condom, put your clothes back on, walk out the door and never look back. This man is a scumbag.

The right person will move to your beat and will never pressure you to do something that you don't want to do. Anytime that you say "no," a man must respect this.

RED FLAG 57: He's selfish in bed

There is nothing worse than a selfish partner in the bedroom - also known as a 'Pillow Prince', this man is only thinking about his pleasure and not yours.

I find a lot of women have more horror stories than good when it comes to sex. It usually starts with the fact that the majority of men don't know where the clitoris is, or that they love to finish the deed in less than 20 seconds.

If you're sleeping with a guy who slides off you after humping you like a hyperactive puppy, then he's probably the kind of a guy who'd talk about himself for hours, let alone leave you to sleep in the wet patch. Selfishness during sex can also be an indication that there are larger underlying problems such as a personality disorder and control issues. If he's selfish in bed, it's a red flag that shouldn't be ignored...

Of course, not everyone is a porn star when it comes to sex and some men will need a bit of guidance. It's important that you communicate your needs. Don't get me wrong, the first time you have sex with someone, it's always a bit awkward and you're probably working eachother out more than aiming for the big O. But if the guy you're with isn't putting his back into it and placing his pleasure above your own, then get rid of him, ASAP.

RED FLAG 58: He becomes distant after sex

Let's imagine this. You've been dating a guy when you decide to take the plunge and have sex with him. You both finish the deed and as you go to snuggle up to him, he quickly jumps up out of bed and starts getting dressed. He says he needs to go to work and that you need to go home. You sense he's acting aloof but you try not to overthink it. He drops you home and you don't hear from him for a couple of days. That is until he calls, asking for you to come over again. *Great!* You head over to his house and once in his bedroom, you both do the deed again. After your rumble and tumble, you notice he is dismissive, and you can sense he's distancing himself from you again. So, what's going on? I asked four of my male friends to explain some of the reasons why men become distant after sex. This is what they said:

Joe: I'm either not interested in taking things further or I've got what I wanted so I don't need to put in the effort anymore.

Alex: It's usually because I'm not into her or just see the relationship as purely sex.

George: It's my way of trying to not get the girl attached. When I don't want anything serious, I keep myself at a distance so she doesn't catch feelings.

Archie: Even if I do like hanging out with someone, if I pull away it's because I don't want her thinking there could be a chance of anything more serious.

So you've heard it from a very small sample of men. There appears to be a correlation in that when a man isn't interested in the long haul he will reduce contact and become distant. Some men may completely distance themselves and ghost you. While others may keep popping back up.

If you face this situation but are happy for a no-strings relationship, then feel free to keep your bedroom door wide open and enjoy the fun. Just don't get your hopes up that a man will change his hot and cold behaviour. He won't.

A man who is looking for long-term commitment (and not just sex) will show you he means business by his actions. If at any point you're questioning his agenda, feel confused or if he becomes distant, then take this as your sign to go.

CHAPTER 7: INSECURITIES, MANIPULATION & CONTROL

I'd like to share a personal story about a man who I dated and loved with all my heart. This man was the love of my life and I would have done anything for him. I was completely and utterly devoted to our relationship from the moment we first met. I wanted nothing more than to be with this person and I made sure I did anything I could to keep it that way. Little did I know, I was selling my soul to the devil.

After six months of being together, I noticed a change in him. He became dismissive and would criticise my every move. From the way I dressed to how I spoke. What he once found endearing about me, now annoyed him. Instead of addressing his behaviour, I made it my mission to appease him.

Whenever he highlighted something negative about me, I would do what I could to change it. From losing weight to not hanging out with my friends, I did what he asked. I was frightened to lose him and would tell myself that I would never find anyone better. I was completely and utterly deluded.

Over time, his control worsened. He kept a tracker on my phone so he could watch my every move. He banned me from the gym and asked me to quit my modelling job, as he didn't like the idea of 'pervy photographers' working with me. I convinced myself that his domination was an act of care, but deep down, I knew something wasn't right. Eventually his verbal and emotional abuse turned physical.

I became a shell of my former self and lived in constant fear of him. Terrified that I would do something to make him unhappy or jeopardise our relationship. What was confusing, is some days he could be loving and kind. Then other days, he acted as if he hated me. It was like living with Jekyll and Hyde.

Our relationship thankfully came to an end, when something inside of me clicked. I had enough of his abuse and knew I had to leave. I took all of my belongings, left his home and never spoke nor saw him again.

Unfortunately, domestic abuse is common. Which is why it's so important that we all educate ourselves on the signs to look out for when letting people into our personal space. The signs are not always obvious. Abuse can be anything from mind games to a physical attack.

It can also be difficult to spot an abuser at the beginning of the relationship. It's once they have you hooked and you've fallen madly in love, when they begin their abuse and manipulation.

This is why I continuously advise biding your time when it comes to dating. Observe their behaviour and most importantly, make yourself your number one priority.

When you start dating someone new, continue doing the things that you love. Surround yourself with good people and follow your passions. The right person will support you.

For those who are in an abusive relationship or believe someone is vulnerable, please seek support from your GP, a mental health specialist or use the domestic violence helplines at the back of this book. If you are in immediate danger do not hesitate to contact your local emergency services.

RED FLAG 59: He gets angry easily

We all get angry from time to time but when someone can't control their emotions, this is a red flag that shouldn't be taken lightly.

Anger is a basic emotion that everyone feels occasionally. However when a person loses control or directs their anger at you or indirectly, this is a red flag that they are dealing with deep-seated turmoil which could escalate.

Never tolerate verbal or physical abuse from anyone. Nor accept intentional property damage such as punching a hole in the wall. While throwing objects or breaking your items won't directly hurt you, this is a clear sign that someone can't control their emotions, which could lead to them physically harming you. No one should ever feel unsafe and if you are in immediate danger call the emergency services.

It's important that you never blame yourself for a person's behaviour. It is their responsibility to control their emotions and how they react. **It doesn't matter if they are calm mannered 99% of the time; if they lose control or direct abuse at you, this is unacceptable and their behaviour is likely to continue or get worse.**

If you are being mentally and emotionally abused, it's important that you talk to your friends, family or your GP about your situation. Alternatively please check the information I have included at the end of this book for advice and support.

RED FLAG 60: He makes you feel insecure

When you are in a healthy relationship, you should feel loved, supported and cared for. **Dating a guy who makes you feel insecure about how you look, your intelligence, or what he's doing when you're not together, is a terrible idea. You deserve more.**

Of course, it's not always someone else's fault for why you feel wobbly. Sometimes feelings of insecurity can come from within. So it is wise that when you do feel insecure to reflect and determine where these feelings are coming from. Is it from past experience? The need for validation? Or is it because the man you're dating isn't reassuring you?

If it's the latter, work out what exactly is causing you to feel negative. If you feel comfortable, share it with your man, see how he reacts. A high quality man will want to resolve and discuss the issue. If your man doesn't, then this is a red flag.

While there's nothing wrong with a little bit of constructive criticism, there's also a fine line between trying to give someone advice and making them feel bad about themselves. Seriously, why would you want to date someone who cannot make you feel good about yourself? Being with someone who makes you feel insecure is torture.

You owe it to yourself to be happy and comfortable in your relationship. If you feel unhappy or that your self-esteem is made worse by the rat you are dating, then you need to put him back into the sewer where he came from.

RED FLAG 61: He checks your phone

For some people, the temptation to look through their partner's phone (especially when they know they would never find out) is incredibly tempting. But just because you can access their texts, Instagram messages and emails all within a few seconds, doesn't mean that you should.

As you might expect, this kind of behaviour often points to a lack of trust in the relationship and checking your partner's phone only feeds distrust into the relationship. If your man feels the need to snoop on your phone or even asks you to look through your messages, then this is a red flag that there is a problem with trust, communication and/or intimacy.

Not only is checking someone's phone an invasion of privacy, it could be a sign that your man has low self-esteem, controlling tendencies or is too immature to be in a relationship. Now that doesn't sound like husband material to me...

Of course, in some relationships, both partners may mutually agree to give each other free rein to check each other's phones. This arrangement can work well for some couples. That said, if you want to maintain privacy, this is perfectly reasonable and your partner must respect that.

RED FLAG 62: He's a jealous guy

It's normal to feel jealous from time to time but when jealousy becomes out of control or possessive, this is a neon red flag.

Contrary to popular belief, jealousy isn't a sign of love or protection. It's a sign of insecurity and low self-worth.

Jealousy can show up in many different ways. A jealous guy may turn up at your girls' night out unannounced to "see how you are" or he may become angry or dismissive whenever you speak to another male (or female). Don't put up with this nonsense.

Men who can't control their jealousy, will *always* be difficult to contend with. And in some cases, men with jealousy issues may try to control or manipulate you. **Life is too short to date someone who can't trust you or those around you, and mild jealousy can develop into something much worse.**

RED FLAG 63: His way or the highway

Dating isn't easy. You will find in every relationship, whether platonic or romantic, there will be a difference of opinion or belief. It can be as simple as deciding where to go for dinner or as complex as how to raise children. Whatever the reason, you will find yourself crossing the bridge of compromise more than once when it comes to your relationships.

The way that you compromise with each other is a complicated balance to get right. It's so common to see a woman ignore her own needs and bend over backwards for someone else. This only leads to resentment and frustration down the line, which is why it's important for couples to meet in the middle.

This can take time to navigate but as long as the end goal is to please each other, you will find a way and work it out. **If for whatever reason, your man isn't willing to meet you in the middle, then you need to stop wearing his red flag as a dress.**

Compromise is all about give and take, and if he's not respecting your needs, this isn't healthy. It's also not healthy when a man wants you to compromise on issues that are fundamental to your own identity or values. If you find yourself in this situation, you need to walk away.

RED FLAG 64: He's controlling

Possessive and controlling men can be difficult to spot at first, as they usually mask their behaviour as protective. This isn't to say all caring and kind individuals should be tarnished with the red flag brush, however it's best to be aware that protective traits can lead to controlling behaviour.

When I was in an abusive relationship, my partner was obsessed with my whereabouts. His 'overprotective' nature led to him putting a tracker on my phone. Despite not wanting to share my location, I naively allowed him to do so. But this only fuelled him to stalk and question my every move. Of course, it's fine to share your location on 'Find my friends' if you both consent and it's coming from a place of concern and care. However if it ever feels suffocating or if he's pressuring you to share your location, run.

The desire to control a person is an incredibly dangerous personality trait. Crippled with insecurities and deep-rooted issues, these individuals need to be avoided like the plague.

If at any point, the man you're dating tries to stop you from doing anything that you want to, tells you what to wear, where to go, what to eat, or who to hang out with, then you need to run for the hills. A healthy relationship is all about supporting each other and wanting your partner to grow, not suffocate them.

RED FLAG 65: He gaslights you

The term "gaslighting" comes from the 1938 book *Gaslight*, where a husband uses trickery to intentionally drive his wife insane in order to steal from her. To doubt her own perception he starts with the simple act of moving objects and dimming the gas-fuelled house lighting. Unaware of her husband's insidious abuse, the wife begins to believe she is going insane.

Although this move is fiction, gaslighting is extremely common in dysfunctional relationships. It's the act of deliberately manipulating a person in such a way that they question their own thoughts, memories, and sanity. It's an abusive tactic aimed to convince the person being gaslit to not trust their own instincts or thoughts.

There are lots of different ways people can gaslight you. Lying is a classic gaslighting sign, where an abuser will lie to you, despite the fact *you* know they are lying. As a result, you start to question yourself and your version of events. A person who is gaslighting may also use the withholding technique, where they may refuse to listen to you or may accuse you of being the one trying to confuse things. The gaslighter may also deny that they ever said or did something you know they did. Again, this discredits your memory and makes you question yourself.

If you are being gaslighted, you may find yourself anxious and constantly apologising to your partner for your thoughts or reactions. You may also feel that you are no longer the person you used to be.

Gaslighting can take a significant toll on your self-esteem and mental health. It's important to remind yourself how healthy relationships should work.

A healthy relationship should have honesty, trust, and communication. Your man should be respectful and supportive to you. If your relationship is missing these basic qualities, it's time to bounce.

RED FLAG 66: He's not supportive

One of the nicest things about being in a relationship is being supported by your loved one. There is nothing better than having someone who takes an interest in you, picks you up when you're feeling down and celebrates your successes. If you're reading this right now and thinking, 'my man doesn't do this for me.', then what are you doing dating this creature? **If your partner isn't supporting you, then you'd be better off being single.**

I haven't got much to add in this chapter, other than the importance of finding a man who will support you through the best and worst times. Although beware of men with a Cinderella fetish - who are great when you're in tears, but can't applaud when you get a promotion.

Support in a relationship is what creates cohesion between two people. Support is the pathway to attachment, love, and care. When a man doesn't have your back or is not consistently supportive, it not only renders the relationship, it can leave you feeling vulnerable. Something I know most of you reading this book will not want or be looking for in a partner.

A man may show early signs that he isn't supportive, so make sure you pay attention to his actions. If he's not listening to your difficulties or not making an effort to celebrate your achievements, then it's likely his support is not going to improve further down the line.

Ladies, you need a cheerleader in your life, not an opponent.

RED FLAG 67: He tests you

I went on a couple of dates with a guy who was gorgeous, funny and terribly charismatic. Sadly this story doesn't end well because by date two, I realised he was testing me.

I love banter and joking around more than the next person, however this man was outrightly rude and couldn't help but make negative assumptions about me. "You've obviously slept with a lot of people.". I nearly spat my drink out. Then he started giving me back-handed compliments, "That's a really nice top. It's a shame you wore your hair like that, it would have looked much better if you had your hair down.". Maybe he was right. Maybe the outfit did look better with my locks over my shoulders. However I didn't ask for his opinion. Later that evening, he told me that my lipstick didn't suit my skintone. He then suggested that for our next date I should wear dungarees. *In your dreams mate.* Listen, I admire honesty, but this guy clearly had no issue in making odd asides about me. The final straw was when he told me that he initially thought I wasn't going to be smart, but "thankfully" I exceeded his expectations. I'll give the guy some credit; he was right about my intellect. As the smartest decision I ever made was never seeing him again.

You may think I was being too sensitive however it's uncharitable jabs like this, that abusers, sociopaths and narcissists love to make at people. These abusers love nothing more than saying blunt or obtuse statements in an attempt to destabilise you. It's a test, to see whether you will stand up for yourself, or whether you will try and reclaim their kindness or affection. They are doing this to work you out and to see if you can be their next victim. **If you have weak boundaries, you are more vulnerable for sociopaths to target and abuse.**

Be aware of this when dating, especially if someone makes cruel statements as this can signal the wilful or absent-minded removal of the mask.

RED FLAG 68: He gives you the silent treatment

When I was in an abusive relationship, my boyfriend would ignore me for days. Experiencing this on a regular basis was frustrating, upsetting and cruel, to say the least. Once he had felt that he had punished me enough or I was practically begging on my knees asking him to talk to me, he would then stop giving me the silent treatment. Eventually we would make amends but it was always on his terms.

Since having therapy and training as a therapist myself, I now know that using the silent treatment is an unproductive way of communicating. While it can sometimes be a form of self-protection, at other times, it can be emotional abuse.

If you find yourself begging for your partner to speak to you, their silence lasts for a long period of time, or the silence only ends when they decide it does. These are red flags that you could be in an emotionally abusive relationship. You may need to seek further outside support if this is the case, as emotional abuse will not only affect your mental health, their behaviour could turn to physical abuse.

If you believe the silent treatment from your partner is not a larger pattern of abuse, you can give them a cooling down period before getting together to resolve the issue.

Sometimes remaining silent can be a positive thing, especially if it keeps people from saying things they might later regret. Other times, silence is unhealthy and can become a pattern of destructive behaviour. When this happens, it becomes a control tactic and this is the point where you should throw in the towel and call it quits.

CHAPTER 8 - MONEY

The subject of money can be a difficult topic to discuss with just about anyone, especially your loved one. While it can be a taboo subject, money will come up at some point in your relationship. Whether that's deciding who will pick up the drinks tab or splitting house bills, the subject of money will rear its head.

The reality is that you and your partner are both different individuals, who will likely have different views on money. For some people, money isn't meant to be saved and should be spent as fast as they get it. Whereas others will constantly save for a rainy day that never comes. Then there are people who are overly generous and spend their hard earned cash like it's going out of fashion. Then you have the other spectrum of humans who would never dream of putting their hand in their own purse or wallet.

Despite the differences in view, when it comes to dating and finances it's important to be open with your partner and vice versa. Although money-related conversations tend to come much later in a relationship, there is no harm in asking questions that will give you an indication as to whether or not you and your man are compatible when it comes to cash management.

As tempting as it is to ask someone, How much do you earn? Do you have debt? Are you asset-rich? These questions are invasive - especially at the beginning of getting to know someone. Until trust has been built and you are both open to discuss money in more detail, it's important to be careful with how you approach this subject. This goes for your partner too. While it's fine to ask if he is good at saving or a big spender, it's not OK to ask how much he has saved or what his current bank balance looks like.

Not everyone is a money wizard and that's OK, however it's good to get an understanding from the early days, if there are going to be any financial issues for your relationship down the road. Let's face it, there's a big difference between not having a stock portfolio and hiding your credit card bills into a shoebox under your bed.

Couples are often faced with the question of do we split bills and how do we navigate financial imbalances as well as expenses? To be honest, this is a conversation that needs to be discussed and (maybe) negotiated. You may feel strongly that your partner pays the majority of the bills because he earns more than you. This is only something you and your partner can work out. Compromise plays a part here and if one of you is not happy with the answer, then you need to reassess your finance plans until you come to an agreement.

Yes, money-handling is a difficult area, but strong communication is key when working it out.

RED FLAG 69: He lives off the bank of mum and dad

Times are hard for millennials and Gen Z. For many of us, we will struggle to afford buying our first homes, let alone live debt free. So it's no wonder that loans are on the rise, whether that's from the Bank of England or the Bank of Mum and Dad.

Borrowing money from your parents isn't inherently wrong, but if the guy you are dating literally lives off his parents, that's not a great sign.

Take this made-up man and situation for an example: a guy you've been dating for a few months has a nice car, apartment, Netflix account and phone bill, all paid for by mum and dad. Does it make him a bad person? Not at all. However it does make him more likely to be a man-child, who only relies on his parents to survive. **If his parents are paying for everything, it probably means that they have a significant amount of control over his life too.**

There's also a risk that this man is either terribly spoiled or has no concept of handling money, which in turn means he's not mature or responsible. Of course, if you don't mind paying all of his bills and everything in between, then this won't be a red flag for you. However, if you're looking for a partnership and not to babysit a grown man, then perhaps you should consider dating his dad.

RED FLAG 70: He asks you for money

While every situation and relationship is different, lending someone money can be a slippery slope to being a lender who never gets their money back.

With this in mind, I'd advise anyone who is to lend money, to ask themselves this before reaching for their purse: *if I don't get my money back, will this put me in a worse financial position?* If the answer is yes, then do not lend anyone money.

Think of it like this. When on a flight we are told by the cabin crew, that in an emergency, when the oxygen masks drop down, you must fit your mask first before helping others. **You can't help others to survive, if you are starving of oxygen. Use this same theory when lending money, time, energy or love.**

In the early stages of dating, if someone asks you to lend them money, I would be on high alert. Regardless of whether you have the cash to give or not, you should put your foot down and set your boundary. Make it clear that you are not a walking bank: *"Unfortunately, I can't lend you money right now, but if you are struggling financially, perhaps we can look at other options?"*.

Remember, a man's situation or inability to handle his finances, is not your responsibility. If he starts to guilt trip or pressure you into lending him money, do a Craig David and walk away.

RED FLAG 71: He is irresponsible with money

How you wish to spend your own money is entirely up to you. The same goes for the person you are dating. If they want to spend their paycheck on shoes or holidays, then so be it. There is nothing wrong with how your partner chooses to spend his hard-earned cash, however if they are burning money and not paying bills or debt, then this is a red flag they are not financially responsible.

Not sure if your man is financially responsible, answer these questions.

Does your man always borrow money from friends, family or you?
Does he exclusively rely on credit cards?
Does he lie about his finances and what he's spent?
Does he splurge on fancy things but struggles to live debt free or pay off bills?

Is he cagey when you discuss finances?
Does he spend big when he gets paid and then struggle for the rest of the month?
Does he not have savings or a pension?

If you answered yes to most of these questions, it is likely your man is financially irresponsible.

This is an issue that won't be resolved overnight and if you're not careful, his irresponsibility could cause detrimental issues to your own finances. Be wary that a man's lack of responsibility in the early stages of your relationship will eventually put a strain on your relationship and bank account.

Whatever you do, don't get a joint account with a man who is financially irresponsible. It's one thing to date someone irresponsible, it's a whole other to let him wreck your credit rating.

While we can all make mistakes and encounter occasional financial problems, if your man is consistently irresponsible - take note. If you're at the stage of living together, this should be an even bigger red flag because ongoing financial problems can be a sign that your man isn't prioritising you or is lacking maturity to gain self-control. Talk to him about helping him to get a better grip with his finances. **If he can't get his shit together, then it's time for you to go.**

RED FLAG 72: He buys your love

Who doesn't love receiving a present? In fact, gifts are a lovely act of kindness. For some people, gift-giving is how they show their love and care for someone, so it may seem strange that gift-giving is a red flag.

But in the words of J-LO 'Love don't cost a thing' and she is absolutely right. Or at least her songwriter is. Unfortunately, when a person gives you too many gifts or buys your love through the power of presents, this can be a sign of love bombing or overcompensating for something they are lacking. While it's totally normal to want to spoil the person you are dating, it's worth being vigilant as to whether they are doing this for you, or it's a power move for them.

If the gift bearer is doing this as a love bombing tactic, then you are very likely to have the gifts he's bought you, thrown back in your face sooner than later. I'm sure some of you have dated a guy where he uses the line: 'With everything I've ever done for you and you treat me like this!', straight after you've confronted his poor behaviour. Gifts from people like this are usually a result of manipulation.

Also look out for lines like, *"After everything I have done for you, I'd expect you to at least do X/Y/Z for me"*. No matter what this man has done for you, you don't need to repay him. That isn't love. This is a form of controlling behaviour and he is using gifts to mask that.

Gifts should be given with no expectation of something in return. If your partner is buying your love and expecting his 'act of kindness' to be reciprocated or idolised, then please start refusing his gifts and walk away. Maybe even run.

RED FLAG 73: He's not generous

There's a very fine line between being careful with how you spend your money and harvesting cobwebs in your wallet. When a man refuses to pay for a can of coke for you, it might be because he can't afford it or simply because he is a tight bastard. If it's the latter, then dealing with someone who is mean with their money will be difficult to deal with in the long-term.

Not being generous is a red flag, as it's a sign he is selfish and unkind. This is not the type of person you want to be in a relationship with. Someone who doesn't have much money can still compensate by making small, thoughtful romantic gestures.

Before we shoot anyone down for not being a big spender, there may be good reasons as to why he is overly-cautious with his money. It could be his upbringing or that he doesn't wish to invest his money on you or when he's with you. If you're a kind and giving person, this may be incredibly frustrating to deal with.

His reasons for being as tight as a duck's arse may be excusable, however if you find he wants you to pay for everything or he can't even give you his last rolo, then it's best that you call it a day with him. Just don't forget to take your purse with you.

RED FLAG 74: He constantly tells you how successful he is

I support anyone who is ambitious, driven or successful. I think it's a wonderful thing when someone is passionate about what they do and is a success because of it. However I draw the line at boasting.

There is an old saying that goes, '**The more someone brags, the less they have**'. While this may not be the case for everyone, I do believe there is an element of truth to this. Why would someone who is successful feel the need to excessively talk about what they have done or own? Why would they feel the need to prove themselves? The same applies to people who compare their wealth against other people.

I dated a guy who wouldn't stop talking about how successful he was and how much money he earned. His gloating went as far to tell me that he owned a collection of properties and classic cars all worth millions. I later discovered that he was actually in debt and didn't have a pot to piss in.

People who brag about their personal successes are usually lacking a sense of self-confidence, which is why they use bragging as their medium to cover their insecurities with self-proclaimed achievements. It can also be an indication that the person you're dealing with is a self-absorbed narcissist.

Human behaviour is complex and there are lots of reasons as to why people brag, however I think it's worth remembering that secure people won't talk about how successful they are nor will they feel the need to impress anyone. Instead, they are eager to learn new things from others.

CHAPTER 9 - FAMILY & FRIENDS

Dating begins with partners getting to know each other by spending time together, sharing experiences and exchanging information. As the relationship evolves and becomes more meaningful, some people will want to take the next step and integrate their partner into other aspects of life. This may include introductions to friends and family.

Introducing a romantic interest to your family and friends is not only flattering to your partner, it can also be beneficial to the depth of your relationship as it solidifies your connection in a big way. It's ultimately the next step to progressing the relationship.

While there are no rules as to when you decide to make the introduction, I would advise (like the broken record that I am) to take your time and wait a bit to make that decision. By waiting it can actually help you be more clear on how you feel about the guy you're dating before getting your loved ones' input. Another thing to consider: If there are children involved (for example, if you're introducing your man to your children), you want to be fairly certain of a future with this person before you add your children's feelings into the mix.

A genuine man who's ready to commit and wants to progress the relationship is going to be excited to let you into his circle. However just because he wants to integrate you into his world and vice versa, doesn't mean it's all green flags moving forward. In fact, it could be an opportunity that highlights red flags that you didn't see before.

RED FLAG 75: He hasn't introduced you to his friends or family

You've been dating an awesome guy for a while. Everything seems to be on the straight and narrow, except for one thing: you haven't met his friends and family.

In some cases, there can be cultural differences as to why your boyfriend isn't introducing you to their friends and family. Maybe he doesn't have a good relationship with his family or fears the drama of his parents' relationship. However, if a guy isn't taking steps to introduce you to his loved ones, then he could be 'stashing' you.

'Stashing' is when someone keeps you away from their inner circle, because they either think the relationship isn't going anywhere or they're holding out for someone better. If you sense this could be why you haven't met his friends and family, then you need to drop him.

To be part of someone's life, you need to integrate into it. If your man isn't encouraging

that, then it's probably because he doesn't see a future with you.

If you want to give him the benefit of the doubt, you can ask him why he hasn't made the introduction. Maybe there's a circumstance you aren't aware of. It's okay to give him a chance to explain, but just make sure he provides a valid reason and not an excuse that is total bullshit.

RED FLAG 76: He hates your friends and family

We can't all get along or be best friends with everyone, however when it comes to your friends and family it's important that your boyfriend likes them.

If your boyfriend can't stand your friends or your family, be cautious of this behaviour, as this could be a sign that he's trying to control and isolate you from your loved ones. **If you think your boyfriend is controlling then you need to dump his ass.**

This behaviour can be subtle to begin with and is likely to happen later in the relationship rather than earlier. If you're unsure if his behaviour is controlling, watch how he reacts when you share stories about other people. Does he roll his eyes or ignore you? Does he demand that you stop hanging out with your family? Does he insult your friend, saying that she's a bad influence?

A controlling partner will also put pressure on you to cut ties with your loved ones. Never do this. Isolating you will make it easier for him to control and manipulate you. Save yourself from misery and leave this jerk.

A good partner will support you and your inner circle, whether that's by attending boring family events with you or talking to your dad about football, even though he doesn't watch it. A good guy will make that effort for you.

RED FLAG 77: He doesn't respect your privacy

I dated a guy who used to love divulging my secrets and our intimate details to his friends and anyone who cared to listen. Not only was this humiliating, it was a breach of trust.

Of course, the majority of guys will talk to their friends about you, and for the most part - that's a good sign. It's when a guy reveals details that you never wanted him to share, when it becomes an issue.

If you find that your partner has been sharing your personal information, call him out on it. If you wish to proceed dating him, establish clear boundaries in the relationship. "Anything I share with you that is in confidence, needs to remain between you and I.". If he continues to cross your boundaries and share your secrets, it's time to end the relationship.

How can you possibly trust or confide in someone who continuously broadcasts your secrets to the world?

This untrustworthy and disrespectful behaviour is unacceptable. **Love without trust, is no love at all.**

RED FLAG 78: He prioritises his friends over you

Relationships are all about compromise. A good partner will understand the importance of balance. He will know to give you free rein to do your own thing as well as make the effort to spend time with you.

This may mean he will spend some weekends with friends. Which is a good thing because time with his friends will keep him sane. Plus it also gives you space to see your friends too. However if a man is prioritising his friends over you, that's when you need to worry.

If a guy is putting his friends first and not including you in his social life, then this is a bad sign. **While it might be 'bros before hoes' for some guys, the man you want to settle down with, shouldn't think like this.**

If you find yourself begging for his time or attention, then I have news for you: it's too late. This guy is taking you for granted and can't be bothered to prioritise you. I'm not sure if your man has the maturity of a teenager or whether he can't stand spending time with you. Either way, he's waving a red flag in your face.

Make yourself a priority and wish this guy well with his future endeavours.

RED FLAG 79: Your friends and family hate him

So your friends and family have met your man and they don't like him. Now what?

This can be an incredibly difficult position to be in, especially when you are feeling loved up and content. However it's worth reminding yourself that your family and friends are protective and want what's best for you.

Now this isn't to say their judgment is correct but they could be seeing something about your partner that perhaps you can't see with rose tinted glasses. Maybe they're speaking from experience or your man did something that was unacceptable, like getting drunk at your cousin's wedding and snogging one of the bridesmaids. Whatever the reason, it's wise to ask your loved ones what it is that they don't like about your partner. Of course, it's important to not get influenced by their opinions, however if your family and friends' reasons are valid or coming from a good place, you should perhaps look at the bigger picture.

Play devil's advocate. Put yourself in their shoes and consider if you would be happy with a friend or family member dating this guy. If one person doesn't like your relationship, then maybe it's just their problem. But if no one in your close circle supports your relationship, then maybe the problem isn't them, it's him.

RED FLAG 80: He's overly attached to his family

If the guy you're dating is overly attached to his family, this is a red flag sign for unnecessary issues ahead. By overly attached I mean examples like your man's family can't stop intruding in his life or he can't make a decision without running to them first. While this may work for some people, if you would rather keep your relationship private and not have people meddling in your life, then this isn't going to work for you.

To cut to the chase, your boyfriend is unlikely to change in the near future, if at all. Getting married and/or having kids will only increase your potential in-laws' involvement in your life. You could ask him to set boundaries with his folks but the likelihood is if he's overly attached, he's not going to set boundaries if he doesn't want to. He may also believe that by drawing an invisible line with his family may cut ties, whether that's financially or emotionally.

An inappropriate relationship with his family, i.e sharing personal details about you, is not only humiliating but will drive you insane eventually. If he's the type who constantly seeks his parent's advice before consulting you or asking for your thoughts, then this is a red flag in itself, because he is ultimately making it clear that he doesn't value your opinion.

Your choices are to either accept that he won't cut the cord or leave.

RED FLAG 81: He hates his family

When you first start dating someone, if he mentions that he doesn't get along with his family, you may think, "That's not a huge deal. Everybody thinks their family is crazy." but when a man truly despises his family, this definitely needs to be explored.

Not everyone feels a close connection to their families. In some cases, people may hate their family for good reason. Perhaps his sibling is evil or one of his parents did something unforgivable. However if you find that your man can't stand his family for reasons that aren't exactly valid, then pay close attention to this red flag.

Are there great guys out there who have a non-existent relationship with their family? Of course. But when they have hatred towards people for no real reason, it's likely they won't be able to be consistent in your relationship either and may end up resenting you for reasons that aren't worth fretting over.

CHAPTER 11: COMMITMENT

Commitment-phobes can be one of the hardest red flags to spot. On one hand you have men who will tell you that they aren't looking for longevity, whereas on the other hand, you have men who display all the right signs of commitment - like moving in with you - but won't put a ring on it!

People view commitment differently. To some it may be marriage and to others it may simply be stating the exclusivity of the relationship to one another. Whichever way you look at commitment, it's important that both you and your partner are on the same page. If you want to be exclusive but your man thinks you should keep things as they are or casual, then you have a problem.

The reality is that when a man claims to have commitment issues or doesn't want to put a label on the relationship, believe him. Do not entertain men like this or delude yourself into thinking you can change his mind. This is wasted energy and time.

It's a myth that commitment issues always arise out of fear. Someone's upbringing, family history, or other factors can also influence how someone behaves in a relationship. Either way, the bottom line is this: **if a man wants to commit to you, he will. If he doesn't, you need to move on and date men who want to lock *you* down.**

RED FLAG 82: He discusses future plans (without you)

Repeat after me: if he doesn't make plans with me, we do not have a future together.

Let's face it, when a guy doesn't include you in his plans or even discusses what the future looks like for you as a couple, then your future together isn't looking too bright!

If you're thinking *'Surely he must be invested if he's sticking around?'.* I would strongly advise that you don't take his presence as commitment. Especially if he isn't discussing the future with you. His lack of plans could be down to not wanting to commit or is simply keeping you around until someone else comes along. I know that's harsh to read but it's true.

So, what's a girl to do? Talk to him and gauge whether he sees the relationship as long-term. If he wants to continue having a casual relationship then you have your answer. **Ditch him. Close this chapter and rewrite your story because I can bet my bottom dollar, you're not included in his happily ever after.**

RED FLAG 83: All of his previous relationships have been short or casual

Men who are not ready to take the leap and commit have the word "casual" in their heads on repeat. If 'casual' comes out of his mouth, make the decision to respond with, "Au revoir!"

Men who reiterate how casual everything was between them and the women they've previously dated, is usually their way of politely expressing to you that they're not ready for a serious relationship. Never ignore these red flags if you are looking for commitment.

The same applies for dating a man who has only been in short relationships. This is a sign he is not a very committed man or he's in his early twenties and exploring. In my experience men who cannot maintain a long-term relationship are either womanziers or do not have the patience or need to put effort into one.

History repeats itself; if his past relationships have all been casual or short-term, the likelihood is you will join that list too.

RED FLAG 84: He refuses to be exclusive

Indecision is a decision. Read that again.

Never act exclusive with a guy who is still keeping his options open. While most men won't sit you down and tell you that you have officially qualified for the girlfriend stage, you can tell when someone is serious about you. Whether that's introducing you as their girlfriend or putting high effort into your relationship, these are all signs he's into you.

Emotionally unavailable men or players, love to pull out the 'I'm not ready for a relationship' card and if this happens to you, do not try to convince him that he should be with you or that you'll wait for eternity until he decides what he wants. **No, we've got shit to do ladies and dating a timewaster is not one of them. If he wants to be with you, he'll be sure, and so will you.**

Another red flag sign that your relationship isn't progressing is if you feel confused about where you stand. **That feeling of limbo is your gut instinct telling you something is off.** Listen to your intuition and remind yourself of your standards and your relationship needs. I'm pretty sure that you didn't write 'a man who refuses to commit' in your green flag list. So don't accept this red flag behaviour. To put it simply, leave.

Never take a man's refusal to commit personally. Sometimes men don't want to commit to you because they live off the gratification of other women, or just because they're not ready to settle down. For some people, an open, polyamorous or ethically non-monogamous relationship is a great thing. But if that's not what you want, then don't hang around.

The same applies if you date a guy who continually ghosts you and then comes back. This push and pull behaviour are common traits of fuck boys and abusers. Unless the guy comes back with some serious explaining and demonstrates they have changed, do not waste your time. When a man keeps you in limbo it not only leaves you feeling confused, your self-esteem will end up on the floor. Don't do it to yourself. **Don't allow a man to come back into your life after they discarded you the first time. He is playing with you and your emotions. Do yourself a favour and tell a fuck boy to fuck off!**

RED FLAG 85: He's a flake

Do not tolerate a man who can't keep to their word. Reliability is a very attractive quality in a person. When someone keeps to their promise, it shows maturity and responsibility. A man who decides to constantly ditch a woman at the eleventh hour is just a waste of time. He is not mature enough, nor is he reliable. Of course, we can all make mistakes but if a guy lets you down more than once, you should show him to the door.

Why? Because flakey behaviour indicates they are not serious about you.

I'm sure you know how frustrating it is when someone flakes on you, so imagine dating a man who isn't reliable? This will turn even the most patient woman insane. This man is incapable of looking after himself, let alone you, so why entertain him?

High-quality men will want to prioritise you and will never make promises they are incapable of keeping. They will do anything in their power to make you feel valued. That means they'll never be late or cancel on you. **You deserve someone you can rely on. Never settle for less.**

RED FLAG 86: He's taken

I'm pretty sure I don't need to go into too much detail as to why dating a married or taken man is a bad idea.

While I understand it's possible to meet someone you find desirable (even when they are off the market), dating a man who has already built his life with another woman often ends badly.

It's a tale as old as time: women date 'taken' men in hope he will leave his partner for them. The truth is, it doesn't matter if he loves you more than he loves her. Homewrecking is immoral and even if you do end up together, it will never be smooth sailing.

Leaving his wife or girlfriend will never be an easy transition. This man is likely to have legal and emotional issues to contend with, not to mention living logistics and possible children to look after. This is not a good start for any relationship. And even if you do find a way to avoid all of this, who isn't to say he won't do the same to you and leave you for another side chick?

There are plenty of men who like to keep other women on the side. Don't be one of them. They are taking you for a ride, so don't go along with it. And if a 'committed' man does try to pursue you, tell him this: "Thank you very much, maybe we can pick this back up when you're single. Oh and please don't forget to send my love to the missus!"

RED FLAG 87: He doesn't want to get married (but you do)

Maybe your man isn't sure if he wants to marry you, maybe he doesn't believe in marriage or maybe he has already shown his commitment by buying a house or having children with you. Whatever his reason for not putting a ring on it, if marriage is important to you and it isn't for him, then you're at a stalemate. You have three solutions, either you propose, accept that he will never propose or leave the relationship.

The latter option may not be desirable, however if the idea of marriage is something you truly want, then you need to find someone who is on the same page as you. At the end of the day, it's what is important to you and if marriage means everything to you, then you need to find someone who matches your belief.

There are plenty of ways to be in a committed relationship without marriage, so this is only an issue if marriage is something that you put a lot of value on.

Marriage also shouldn't be a decision made entirely by the man. Yes, it's lovely to be proposed to, but ideally you should both have had lots of discussions about the future you're imagining together long before he takes out his credit card at Tiffany.

RED FLAG 88: He doesn't want kids (but you do)

It's perfectly ok if someone doesn't want children, however if your lifelong dream is to have a family, you will need to find a man who feels the same.

Every couple needs to have the kids talk, sooner rather than later. So, it is only natural that when you find a man that you like, the first thing you want to know is if they're on the same page.

A family may not be on the agenda for you right now, but if it is something you want in the future, it is wise to suss out whether the guy you're dating is a potential family man or a no-baggage kind of guy.

I dated a guy who from as early as the fourth date made it very clear that he didn't want kids. Or at least not until another twenty years. Of course, men can wait for that long. There's no rush for them, whereas us women have the pressure of a biological clock ticking.

Unfortunately, that meant that his life plan didn't match mine and while I didn't want to start planning a pregnancy, I wasn't going to wait twenty years either. The same applies if a guy avoids the topic of kids, instead of giving you a straight answer. **There is nothing wrong with wanting different things, as long as you are both being transparent with each other.**

Final thoughts

I know better than anyone that it's easier said than done when dodging red flags, but I cannot emphasise this enough: **if you allow the wrong man to enter your life, he will get in the way of the right one.** Every time you entertain or chase these idiots, you lose time pursuing someone who wants serious commitment. You lose the opportunity of being with someone who wants you.

I know I've said this continuously throughout the book but take your time when dating and getting to know someone. There really isn't any rush and if they are 'the one', they will be patient and go with your flow, even if you do pump the brakes.

I'm an advocate for trusting your intuition. Your instinct is one of the most powerful tools you have. So use it. If something doesn't make you feel comfortable or you start to question the other person's behaviour, there's a good chance that your red flag radar is working.

You are a woman who deserves all of your green flag boxes to be ticked. I trust that this guide will help you sift through the wrong people and that every time you meet a red flag, you can tell yourself , "He's not the one", and keep it moving until you find 'the one'.

For your convenience, I have made a list of some tips that may be helpful on your journey for avoiding red flags:

- The quickest way to spot a red flag is to pay attention to what a man does rather than what he says. Anyone can give you lip service and tell you all the things you want to hear. A real man will show you. Read that again.

- Don't be afraid to prioritise yourself. Putting your needs first and placing strong boundaries is not something high-quality men will resent. On the contrary, men actually respect it. They'll regard you as a secure woman who knows what she wants and won't allow anything less.

- Stop confusing emotional drama or abuse, for love. Ask yourself, am I really happy with this situation? Is this what I want from a relationship?

- Never settle with someone because you're scared of being alone or worried about your age or status. A relationship with a red flag is far worse than being on your own.

- Don't risk your dignity chasing a man who is not interested or has dumped or ghosted you.

- Stop wasting energy trying to analyse why the man you date behaves the way he does. You may never know. Just accept the fact that he isn't the one, and it's best for you to leave him alone and move on.

- Never lower your standards to accept poor behaviour from a man because of his status or looks. No matter how good looking or great he is on paper, if a man is not kind, doesn't respect or treat you well, he is not worthy of your time.

- Never date in a place of desperation or a need to fill a void. Red flags will smell this from a mile off. Remain self-assured and only date when you are in a good headspace.

- When it comes to dating, you will have to adapt a ruthless approach when filtering the wrong men from your life. It's the only way to avoid abusers, timewasters and fuck boys.

- Find a partner who shares your values, treats you with respect, love and kindness - but most importantly who is your friend and teammate.

- If you believe that you are worthy and deserve what you want, then you are far more likely to attract the man and relationship that you want. Keep your standards high and remember your worth.

- Most importantly, remember to remain positive and enjoy the dating process. Use this time to get to know what you want and what you don't want. For every bad date or relationship, take it as a lesson. For every red flag you filter out, you are one step closer to finding the one.

Help & Support

This page has useful information and links for where to find help for domestic violence and addiction, as well as mental health support.

Please note: this information may have changed as of the date of publishing.

UK support services for domestic violence

If you need to speak to someone:

- **Refuge 24 Hour National Domestic Violence Helpline** – 0808 2000 247
- **Live Fear Free Helpline** (Wales) – 0808 801 800
- **Scotland's 24 Hour Domestic Abuse And Forced Marriage Helpline** (Scotland) – 0800 027 1234
- **Northern Ireland 24 Hour Domestic And Sexual Abuse Helpline** (N Ireland) – 0808 802 1414
- **Karma Nirvana** UK Helpline for honour-based abuse and forced marriage - 0800 5999 247

- **Respect** Guidance for perpetrators – 0808 802 4040
- **The Men's Advice Line** for male victims of domestic abuse – 0808 8010327
- **ManKind Initiative** Helpline for men suffering domestic violence, and their friends and family - 01823334244
- **The Mix** Free information and support for under 25s in the UK – 0808 808 4994
- **Galop** the National LGBT+ Domestic Abuse Helpline – 0800 999 5428
- **Samaritans** 24/7 service – 116 123

Bright Sky app

Bright Sky is a mobile app and website for anyone experiencing domestic abuse, or who is worried about someone else.

The app can be downloaded for free from the app stores. Only download the app if it is safe for you to do so and if you are sure that your phone isn't being monitored.

https://www.hestia.org/brightsky

Women's Aid local support services directory

Women's Aid have a directory of domestic abuse support services across the UK.

If you are experiencing domestic abuse or are worried about friends or family, you can access the Women's Aid live chat service 7 days a week, 10am to 6pm.

helpline@womensaid.org.uk

https://www.womensaid.org.uk/domestic-abuse-directory/

Victim Support

Victim Support run these services for victims and survivors of any abuse or crime, regardless of when it occurred or if the crime was reported to the police:

- free, independent and confidential 24/7 Supportline 08 08 16 89 111
- live chat service
- My Support Space - free online resource

https://www.mysupportspace.org.uk/

Ask for ANI codeword

If you are experiencing domestic abuse and need immediate help, ask for 'ANI' in a participating pharmacy. 'ANI' stands for Action Needed Immediately. If a pharmacy has the 'Ask for ANI' logo on display, it means they're ready to help. They will offer you a private space, provide a phone and ask if you need support from the police or other domestic abuse support services.

Check whether someone has an abusive past

If you are concerned that a new, former or existing partner has an abusive past you can ask the police to check under the Domestic Violence Disclosure Scheme (also known as 'Clare's Law'). This is your 'right to ask'. If records show that you may be at risk of domestic abuse, the police will consider disclosing the information. A disclosure can be made if it is legal, proportionate and necessary to do so.

If you are concerned about a friend or family member, you can apply for a disclosure on behalf of someone you know.

You can make a request to the police for information about a person's previous violent offending in person at the police station or elsewhere, by telephone, by email, online or as part of a police investigation. Support agencies and services can also help you ask the police about this.

Get a court order to protect you or your child

If you're a victim of domestic abuse you can apply for a court order or injunction to protect yourself or your child from:

- your current or previous partner
- a family member
- someone you currently or previously lived with

This is called a non-molestation or occupation order.

You can apply online, by email or by post.

https://www.gov.uk/injunction-domestic-violence

If you are worried that a friend, neighbour or loved one is a victim of domestic abuse, you can call the National Domestic Abuse Helpline for free and confidential advice, 24 hours a day on 0808 2000 247.

Or you can contact the other support services listed on this page.

Seeking help for someone you know can be challenging but #YouAreNotalone. Domestic abuse advisers will offer confidential, non-judgemental information and advice on the options available to you helping you to keep safe and make informed choices.

If you believe there is an immediate risk of harm to someone, or it is an emergency, you should always call 999.

If someone confides in you, there is more information on how to support a friend who is being abused.

https://www.gov.uk/government/publications/domestic-abuse-recognise-the-signs/domestic-abuse-recognise-the-signs#support-a-friend-if-theyre-being-abused

Emergency help

If you are in immediate danger, please call 999 and ask for the police.

If you are not safe to speak, use the Silent Solution system by calling 999 and then pressing 55 when prompted if using a mobile or waiting to be connected through to the police automatically if using a landline.

If you're deaf, hard of hearing or speech-impaired, you can use the textphone service 18000 or text 999 if you've pre-registered with the emergencySMS service.

https://www.relayuk.bt.com/how-to-use-relay-uk/contact-999-using-relay-uk.html

UK mental health support services

Mental health services are free on the NHS, but in some cases you'll need a referral from your GP to access them.

You need to talk to an NHS professional now

Find an NHS urgent mental health helpline (England only)

https://www.nhs.uk/service-search/mental-health/find-an-urgent-mental-health-helpline

You need help now but you do not know where to start

Where to get urgent help for mental health

https://www.nhs.uk/mental-health/advice-for-life-situations-and-events/where-to-get-urgent-help-for-mental-health/

You want help from a mental health charity helpline

Get help from a mental health charity helpline

https://www.nhs.uk/mental-health/nhs-voluntary-charity-services/charity-and-voluntary-services/get-help-from-mental-health-helplines/

You want crisis coping tools

https://www.mind.org.uk/need-urgent-help/

Alternatively contact your GP or a mental health professional for further support.

UK addiction helplines

A GP is a good place to start. They can discuss your problems with you and get you into treatment.

They may offer you treatment at the practice or refer you to your local drug service.

If you're not comfortable talking to a GP, you can approach your local drug treatment service yourself.

Visit the Frank website to find local drug treatment services.

https://www.talktofrank.com/get-help/find-support-near-you

If you're having trouble finding the right sort of help, call the Frank drugs helpline on 0300 123 6600. They can talk you through all your options.

You may be going through further experiences related to addiction and dependency. Further information on trauma, bereavement and support for abuse might be helpful.

https://www.mind.org.uk/information-support/types-of-mental-health-problems/trauma/about-trauma/

https://www.mind.org.uk/information-support/guides-to-support-and-services/bereavement/about-bereavement/

https://www.mind.org.uk/information-support/guides-to-support-and-services/abuse/about-this-resource/

For general information about addiction

Beating Addictions

beatingaddictions.co.uk

Information about a range of addictive behaviours and treatments.

DrugWise

drugwise.org.uk

Information about drugs, alcohol and tobacco.

NHS Live Well

nhs.uk/livewell

Advice, tips and tools to help with health and wellbeing.

For people experiencing addiction

Alcoholics Anonymous (AA)

0800 9177 650

help@aamail.org (email helpline)

alcoholics-anonymous.org.uk

Help and support for anyone with alcohol problems.

Alcohol Change UK

alcoholchange.org.uk

Information and support options for people worried about how much alcohol they are drinking, in both English and Welsh.

Club Drug Clinic

020 3317 3000

clubdrugclinic.cnwl.nhs.uk

Information and support for people worried about their use of recreational drugs. The clinic offers help in the London boroughs of Kensington & Chelsea, Hammersmith & Fulham and Westminster.

Cocaine Anonymous UK

0800 612 0225

helpline@cauk.org.uk

cauk.org.uk

Help and support for anyone who wants to stop using cocaine.

DAN 24/7

0808 808 2234

81066 (text DAN)

dan247.org.uk

A bilingual English and Welsh helpline for anyone in Wales in need of further information or help relating to drugs or alcohol. Also known as the Wales Drug & Alcohol Helpline.

FRANK

0300 123 6600

talktofrank.com

Confidential advice and information about drugs, their effects and the law.

Gamblers Anonymous

gamblersanonymous.org.uk

Support groups for people who want to stop gambling.

Gamcare

0808 8020 133

gamcare.org.uk

Information and support for people who want to stop gambling, including a helpline and online forum.

Marijuana Anonymous

0300 124 0373

helpline@marijuana-anonymous.org.uk

marijuana-anonymous.co.uk

Help for anyone worried about cannabis use.

Narcotics Anonymous

0300 999 1212

ukna.org

Support for anyone who wants to stop using drugs.

National Problem Gambling Clinic

cnwl.nhs.uk/cnwl-national-problem-gambling-clinic

Treats people with gambling problems living in England and Wales aged 16 and over.

NHS Better Health – Quit smoking

nhs.uk/better-health/quit-smoking

NHS information and advice to help stop smoking.

Sex and Love Addicts Anonymous

07984 977 884 (Infoline)

slaauk.org

Support groups for people with sex and love addictions.

Turning Point

turning-point.co.uk

Health and social care services in England for people with a learning disability. Also supports people with mental health problems, drug and alcohol abuse or unemployment.

We Are With You

wearewithyou.org.uk

Supports people with drug, alcohol or mental health problems, and their friends and family.

Adfam

adfam.org.uk

Information and support for friends and family of people with drug or alcohol problems.

Bereaved through Alcohol and Drugs (BEAD)

beadproject.org.uk

Information and support for anyone bereaved through drug or alcohol use.

Families Anonymous

0207 4984 680

famanon.org.uk

Support for friends and family of people with drug problems.

National Association for Children of Alcoholics

0800 358 3456

helpline@nacoa.org.uk

nacoa.org.uk

Provides information, advice and support for anyone affected by a parent's drinking, including adults.

Printed in Great Britain
by Amazon

71199793R00098